M000314477

Management on the Cutting Edge series

Abbie Lundberg, series editor

Published in cooperation with *MIT Sloan Management Review*

The AI Advantage: How to Put the Artificial Intelligence Revolution to Work
Thomas H. Davenport

The Technology Fallacy: How People are the Real Key to Digital Transformation
Gerald C. Kane, Anh Nguyen Phillips, Jonathan Copulsky, and Garth Andrus

Designed for Digital: How to Architect Your Business for Sustained Success
Jeanne W. Ross, Cynthia M. Beath, and Martin Mocker

See Sooner, Act Faster: How Vigilant Leaders Thrive in an Era of Digital Turbulence
George S. Day and Paul J. H. Schoemaker

Leading in the Digital World: How to Foster Creativity, Collaboration, and Inclusivity
Amit S. Mukherjee

The Ends Game: How Smart Companies Stop Selling Products and Start Delivering Value
Marco Bertini and Oded Koenigsberg

Open Strategy: Mastering Disruption from Outside the C-Suite
Christian Stadler, Julia Hautz, Kurt Matzler, and Stephan Friedrich von den Eichen

The Transformation Myth: Leading Your Organization through Uncertain Times
Gerald Kane, Rich Nanda, Anh Nguyen Phillips, and Jonathan Copulsky

Winning the Right Game: How to Disrupt, Defend, and Deliver in a Changing World
Ron Adner

The Digital Multinational: Navigating the New Normal in Global Business
Satish Nambisan and Yadong Luo

Work without Jobs: How to Reboot Your Organization's Work Operating System
Ravin Jesuthasan and John W. Boudreau

The Future of Competitive Strategy: Unleashing the Power of Data and Digital Ecosystems
Mohan Subramaniam

Productive Tensions: How Every Leader Can Tackle Innovation's Toughest Trade-Offs
Chris B. Bingham and Rory M. McDonald

Working with AI: Real Stories of Human-Machine Collaboration
Thomas H. Davenport and Steven M. Miller

Enterprise Strategy for Blockchain: Lessons in Disruption from Fintech, Supply Chains, and Consumer Industries
Ravi Sarathy

Redesigning Work: How to Transform Your Organization and Make Hybrid Work for Everyone
Lynda Gratton

Inside the Competitor's Mindset: How to Predict Their Next Move and Position Yourself for Success
John Horn

Workforce Ecosystems: Reaching Strategic Goals with People, Partners, and Technologies
Elizabeth J. Altman, David Kiron, Jeff Schwartz, and Robin Jones

Data Is Everybody's Business: The Fundamentals of Data Monetization
Barbara H. Wixom, Cynthia M. Beath, and Leslie Owens

Data Is Everybody's Business

Data Is Everybody's Business

The Fundamentals of Data Monetization

Barbara H. Wixom, Cynthia M. Beath, and Leslie Owens

The MIT Press
Cambridge, Massachusetts
London, England

© 2023 Massachusetts Institute of Technology

All rights reserved. No part of this book may be reproduced in any form by any electronic or mechanical means (including photocopying, recording, or information storage and retrieval) without permission in writing from the publisher.

The MIT Press would like to thank the anonymous peer reviewers who provided comments on drafts of this book. The generous work of academic experts is essential for establishing the authority and quality of our publications. We acknowledge with gratitude the contributions of these otherwise uncredited readers.

This book was set in ITC Stone Serif Std and ITC Stone Sans Std by New Best-set Typesetters Ltd. Printed and bound in the United States of America.

Library of Congress Cataloging-in-Publication Data

Names: Wixom, Barbara Haley, 1969– author. | Beath, Cynthia Mathis, 1944–
    author. | Owens, Leslie (Leslie Ann), 1972– author.
Title: Data is everybody's business : the fundamentals of data monetization /
    Barbara H. Wixom, Cynthia M. Beath, and Leslie Owens.
Description: Cambridge, Massachusetts : The MIT Press, [2023] | Series:
    Management on the cutting edge | Includes bibliographical references and index.
Identifiers: LCCN 2022055462 (print) | LCCN 2022055463 (ebook) |
    ISBN 9780262048217 (hardcover) | ISBN 9780262375351 (epub) |
    ISBN 9780262375344 (pdf)
Subjects: LCSH: Electronic data processing—Economic aspects. | Big data—
    Economic aspects. | Data mining—Economic aspects.
Classification: LCC HF5548.2 .W59 2023 (print) | LCC HF5548.2 (ebook) |
    DDC 658/.05—dc23/eng/20221121
LC record available at https://lccn.loc.gov/2022055462
LC ebook record available at https://lccn.loc.gov/2022055463

10 9 8 7 6 5 4 3 2 1

Contents

Series Foreword

The world does not lack for management ideas. Thousands of researchers, practitioners, and other experts produce tens of thousands of articles, books, papers, posts, and podcasts each year. But only a scant few promise to truly move the needle on practice, and fewer still dare to reach into the future of what management will become. It is this rare breed of idea—meaningful to practice, grounded in evidence, and *built for the future*—that we seek to present in this series.

Abbie Lundberg

Editor in chief
MIT Sloan Management Review

Foreword

When Professor Barbara Wixom (Barb) joined MIT Sloan Center for Information Systems Research (MIT CISR) as a principal research scientist to lead the data research stream, she advocated for an advisory board of senior global data leaders to help her. That's us. Barb needed data experts from a wide variety of organizations to participate in studies, set research priorities, and vet insights. Our charge was to help keep the center's data research relevant, edgy, and applicable.

We share our passion for all things data via chat, while visiting the MIT campus, in executive education sessions, and in virtual meetups. Through these interactions, we have gotten to know and trust Barb, as well as her MIT CISR collaborators, Cynthia and Leslie, and each other. The teamwork and sharing tend to spark ideas and new directions. When one of us has something particularly unique underway, the MIT CISR team investigates what we are doing and helps us find the "aha!" moments. They write up our efforts as a case study when our approach might help others succeed.

In Q1 of 2021, Barb kicked off a virtual conversation for the board called "Inspiring Hearts and Minds." She asked us to reflect: *why is data different today* versus when we all started in the field? And because of that difference, *what should we be doing* as data leaders? She hypothesized that data leaders had to become much more evangelical; she thought we were carrying too much of the responsibility for our organizations' data assets. And, to communicate persuasively, data leaders needed a simple, everyday business language that a broad base of people could understand. We agreed. We felt it too.

In our ensuing conversation, we agreed that data needs to become an expected competence for the majority, an evolution that requires patience, commitment, and ongoing investment in talent and new ways of working. To build and keep momentum, we've found that you need the diverse perspectives (especially regarding customer needs) of a wide range of people, from different functions, disciplines, generations, and levels, who are personally invested.

At this point, we don't need to persuade people that data has value. Instead, we need to help them contribute to the shift from tactical, local efforts to building enterprise-wide capabilities. We've found that when people see data as within their purview (not a responsibility of a few or an IT department), they spot innovation opportunities more readily. As data leaders, we focus on generating and sharing trusted data assets and leading data literacy programs. Ideally, because of our efforts, most of our colleagues will feel comfortable using data to improve work or products.

Many of us already apply MIT CISR research in our organizations and can point to the benefits. Now, we welcome having a book that pulls the research together in a way that appeals to all. We plan to distribute and discuss this book across our organizations, coach others in the easy-to-use frameworks, and inspire our people to participate in data monetization to

- build data assets,
- create novel, data-driven ways of working and customer experiences, and
- learn about data and share knowledge about data with colleagues.

We hope to rally our colleagues across the enterprise—from our front-line employees to our senior leaders and board members—to embrace the idea that data is everybody's business. This book is for everybody.

—MIT CISR Data Research Advisory Board Members

Introduction: Data Is Everybody's Business

Everyone will say that data is extremely important to the business. However, beyond that, people don't know what to do next.

—Mihir Shah, Fidelity Investments

It's common for leaders who want to create value from data to look for inspiration within companies like Google. They might go on a road trip and tour Google's California offices. While there, they might encounter advanced technology and brilliant data scientists developing proprietary artificial intelligence–based products, such as a map that automatically updates when a business is open.[1] But what else is behind a company like Google's success? It's several things. It's the expectation that everybody is a data practitioner, inventing new data-driven work practices and sharing them with others. It's an environment where data has been converted into data assets that people can find, trust, and use to address unmet business needs without having to create manual, bespoke processes and controls. And it's a firm-wide push to convert such data assets into revenues since, after all, the mission of Alphabet Inc. (Google's parent company) is to "organize the world's information and make it universally accessible and useful."[2]

Like newlyweds returning from a fantastic honeymoon, leaders from traditional companies might return to their offices after a field trip to Silicon Valley and feel overwhelmed by what's ahead. Of course, few organizations have as much data as Google. But all organizations, including yours, have lots of data. It can be internal (e.g., accounting data) or external (e.g., purchased data about consumer credit risk or household preferences). It can be structured (e.g., customer orders) or unstructured (e.g., tweets). It could live in a spreadsheet, the cloud of a consultant, an email archive, a data warehouse, or a data lake, to name just a few spots. Organizations today are great at amassing data, causing a data deluge that grows with every technology advancement in storage, processing, electronics, networking, and telecommunications.

Yes, in most organizations, data is everywhere. Yet typically, the data is tied to some context.[3] The data is shaped and constrained by the processes that create it and govern it. It is stuck in closed platforms, replicated in multiple locations, incomplete, inaccurate, and poorly defined. As a result, organizations focus a lot of managerial attention on liberating data from silos and applying it to new specific uses such as calculating customer churn or spotting supply chain breaks. Such efforts are complicated and filled with friction, and each time a new chance to use the data emerges, somebody must overcome the same hurdles. Leveraging data to meet an unanticipated challenge or opportunity seems like a Herculean feat.

Companies like Google take a different approach with their data. They decontextualize data and prepare data assets that can be accessed and reused for innumerable purposes. Such data assets are accurate, complete, current, standardized, searchable, and understandable— assets that everybody across the company can easily incorporate into their value-creating initiatives. The "data" in the title of this book refers to *data assets*. The book will describe how organizations develop data assets so they can be exploited repeatedly.

The use of "everybody" in the title also has significance. Data is not just for people with "data" in their job title. For organizations to develop data assets and exploit them over and over, many more people need to be in the mix. Just as an organization's financial results are the responsibility of more than finance and accounting staff, just as customer retention requires more than sales, and just as talent management is not solely owned by human resources (HR), data responsibilities need to be held well beyond the data teams.

But why does the title say that data is everybody's "business?" Because your organization should be using data to make money and save money. The financial inflows generated from your organization's collective data investments should be larger than your financial outflows. If your organization does not actively manage the amount of money you generate from your data—that is, the extent to which you *monetize* your data—you will limit your financial inflows. Worst case, you will lose money. The concept of data monetization is a fundamental business concept that will be explained in chapter 1.

Clear, Memorable, and Integrated Frameworks

Leaders often find themselves trying to develop people's "data savvy" without much support. Unlike other management topics that are well covered in business schools and executive education, the field of data is relatively new, and standards and core curriculum are still emerging.[4] The Data Management Association, for example, published the first edition of its data management body of knowledge in 2009.[5] As a result, organizations have had to develop their own data training materials, create their own terminology, and engage in a lot of trial and error to get stuff right.

This book offers simple language and integrated concepts that can quickly raise people's data savvy. There are three key frameworks, shown in figure 0.1. After reading this book, any reader should be able to pick up a marker and draw the frameworks on a whiteboard as context for data monetization conversations.

The first framework summarizes the five data monetization *capabilities* organizations use to develop data assets and make data monetization fast and successful: data management, data platform, data science, customer understanding, and acceptable data use. The capabilities are depicted as a fan because they are closely related and work together. Capabilities are the expertise developed from mastering practices to decontextualize data: divorcing it from a specific condition or context and turning it into reusable data assets. This expertise may be embodied

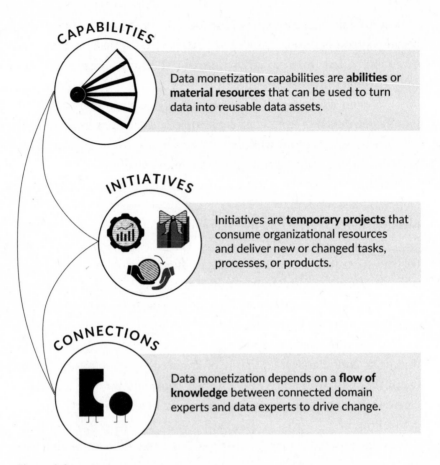

Figure 0.1
Three key data monetization frameworks

in people (as abilities or proficiencies) or in other material resources (tools, routines, technology, forms, policies, and so forth). Over time, data monetization practices build the organization's muscle in the five data monetization capabilities.

The second framework describes three kinds of *initiatives* in which organizations invest that generate financial returns from their data assets: improving work, wrapping products with data-fueled features and experiences, and selling information solutions. Each approach uses data differently and has an ideal owner, a set of risks to mitigate, and unique outcomes. Recognizing what makes these three approaches different is crucially important; trying to run a selling initiative as if it were an improving initiative can be disastrous. It would be like fixing a kitchen appliance with the tools, talent, and expertise needed for landscaping the yard. Organizations that understand the distinct requirements of each data monetization approach can make the right investments, set realistic expectations, and generate optimal returns.

The third framework offers a way to think about organizational design for data monetization. It describes five organizational *connections* between domain experts and data experts. The term *domain* refers to an area of subject matter that is valued in an organization, not including subject matter related to data. (For example, accounting, marketing, nursing, teaching, and law enforcement are common domains.) Organizations can't expect people to embrace and engage with data monetization on their own—think about how busy people are simply trying to keep up with business as usual! To encourage changes in people's behaviors and (ideally) habits, organizations must actively establish connections between domain and data experts so that people share knowledge, learn, and, ultimately, change things. When people across your organization know how to leverage data assets and data monetization capabilities to innovate, and when they participate in and take responsibility for data monetization initiatives, then you know your organization's connections are working.

Collectively, the three frameworks work together. They reinforce each other, working like a flywheel to produce positive momentum that picks up over time. To apply the frameworks, you can begin anywhere. As you better understand and build data monetization capabilities, you enable more and different kinds of initiatives and you engage more people across the organization. As you become more proficient at deploying and generating returns from data monetization initiatives, you satisfy and excite data monetization investors, participants, and benefactors. And as you activate connections between domain and data experts all over the organization, you grow the population of stake-holders who will build and use data monetization capabilities and participate in initiatives.

Who Should Read This Book?

This book is for . . . everybody! That is, everybody who works in an organization. It has been designed to be relevant to audiences at all levels of data expertise and to appeal to people in organizations large and small, commercial and noncommercial, national and global. Yes, even philanthropic and public organizations engage in data monetization. This book can help you—and it can help you help others. It is as relevant to leaders who manage their organization's data monetization strategy as it is to the people who bring data monetization principles to life.

This book is not a list of clever ways to monetize data, although the examples in this book might spark some ideas for you. It bypasses the pros and cons of different data vendors or data architectures. Instead, this book will help you articulate your ideas and move them to fruition. You will learn how to monetize data successfully by focusing on a few essential frameworks.

About the Research

The authors of this book are affiliated with the MIT Center for Information Systems Research (MIT CISR), a global nonprofit research center nested within the MIT Sloan School of Management. Founded in 1974, MIT CISR is committed to helping organizational leaders manage technology (including data) successfully. The center produces relevant academic research for leaders grappling with contemporary technology management challenges.

The academic researchers at MIT CISR seek to identify and understand a phenomenon to explain and predict outcomes. The research behind this book has examined how organizations generate value from data from many angles over several decades. The organizations studied range from ones as large as Microsoft to some as small as thirty-person start-up AdJuggler, as diverse as airlines, high-end retailers, and data aggregators, both commercial and noncommercial, including government agencies and nonprofits, located all over the world. The theoretical foundations of the research focus on organizations and the people in them, not computer science.

MIT CISR research often starts with exploratory qualitative studies—case studies and field observations—to understand the problems organizations have, what solutions work, and what solutions don't. Many of those case studies appear in this book. Qualitative studies are followed by confirmatory quantitative analyses, using interview and survey data. Readers will find the results of those studies in this book. A variety of theories are used to develop the research insights. In some cases, collaborators with deep expertise (from MIT and other universities around the world) help formulate new ideas or extend current thinking; at other times, concepts from the marketing and management literatures are borrowed and reapplied.

The research behind this book was carried out alongside practitioners, data practitioners in particular. In 2015, MIT CISR initiated a data research advisory board of chief data officers and chief analytics officers from MIT CISR member organizations. These one-hundred-plus practitioners not only patiently complete extensive surveys and participate in interviews but also prioritize topics to be studied, debate research findings, and test out frameworks. Their voices can be heard throughout this book.

How This Book Will Unfold

The book opens (chapter 1) by defining data monetization and a few other foundational concepts—such as the *data-insight-action* process, value creation, and value realization—that will reappear throughout the book. Next, chapter 2 describes five enterprise capabilities that organizations need for data monetization to succeed as well as how organizations build these capabilities. Then, three chapters (chapters 3, 4, and 5) give in-depth looks at the three kinds of initiatives you can use to monetize data: improving, wrapping, and selling. You will explore the critical success factors for each data monetization approach and learn how to create and realize value using each one. In chapter 6, you will learn how to engage more people in your organization in the work of data monetization. This work includes creating connections and incentivizing people to interact and reuse data assets. Chapter 7 describes the importance of establishing a data monetization strategy and presents four strategy archetypes representing four different ways to monetize data. Finally, chapter 8 will encourage you to make it your business to monetize data.

Each chapter starts with questions for you to ask yourself. Research findings and definitions of key terms are presented along the way. The chapters offer in-depth case studies that contextualize the purpose and application of the frameworks. Finally, each chapter ends with a Time to Reflect section to help you apply its lessons and concepts to your own situation. Enjoy the read!

1 Data Monetization

If I cannot articulate the value of an initiative in a monetized way, it's a wish list; it's nothing but a wish list.

—Jeevan Rebba, Otsuka Pharmaceutical Companies

Work has changed profoundly in the past few years. Managers are introducing new work practices that help employees innovate, not just punch the clock. For example, customer journey mapping initiatives help people understand customer perspectives and improve customer experiences; design thinking inspires people to solve problems creatively and to enhance products in appealing ways; and test and learn processes support people in taking small risks with small ideas that have the potential to develop into something big.

These new ways of working have created an opening for individual employees to contribute directly to organizational success. Regardless of what team they represent or how senior their role is, employees today are more attentive to how their work impacts the whole organization and how changes to their work might pay off. At CarMax, for example, employees throughout the company can link their work to one of CarMax's missions: either they are trying to sell more cars, or they are trying to buy more cars.[1] As a result of these clear goals, creative people across the company can unleash ideas on how changes to the tasks they perform could help achieve the CarMax mission. A salesperson, for example, could hypothesize that an improvement in how sales leads are identified would get more cars sold, run a local experiment, and demonstrate that the idea worked.

The data assets available to employees at modern organizations like CarMax play a significant role in these new ways of working. Data assets provide a single source of truth; they draw on more data and novel data, often sourced from social media, mobile devices, artificial intelligence (AI), and the Internet of Things (IoT). People at these organizations use data assets to measure, validate, inform, persuade, and prompt—in fiscally and socially responsible ways. Data assets are built to be monetized.

This book features many examples of people in organizations actively pursuing data monetization. In the last decade, Microsoft used data to move its business model from being product based to cloud services based and saw its stock price soar.[2] Banco Bilbao Vizcaya Argentaria (BBVA), a financial services company, used data to become a digital-first financial services provider. As of 2021, it had won Forrester's award for overall mobile banking digital experience in Europe five years in a row.[3] Finally, PepsiCo used data to identify and serve granular market needs and transformed its transactional retailer relationships into collaborative partnerships.[4] These three organizations and their data monetization journeys are featured in detail in chapters 2, 3, and 4, respectively. So, what is data monetization?

Data monetization is turning data into money. Money is a crucial resource for all organizations, public and private. Organizations need money from customers, donors, or citizens, and they need to handle that money prudently. Organizations use data not only to *create* valuable benefits—customer and employee satisfaction, brand capital, desired product enhancements, streamlined processes, or citizen welfare—but also to purposefully *realize* financial value—money—to improve their bottom line.

> Data monetization *is the generation of financial returns from data assets.*

These days, different kinds of organizations pay attention to many different "bottom lines." What number tells the world that your organization is sustainably efficient and effective? It might be your net cash flow, your net income, your unrestricted net income (if you are a nonprofit), or some other measure of efficiency and effectiveness. In this book, bottom line means the difference between money in and money out.

There is a world of difference between creating valuable benefits and turning those benefits into money. We will call the first *value creation*. By that, we mean creating benefits that are desirable and have the potential to reach the bottom line. These benefits are common goals in data initiatives: more streamlined processes, smoother supply chains, employee satisfaction, or products that customers find desirable. This book is mainly about how to create value from data.

We will call the second *value realization*. By that, we mean transforming the value created by these initiatives into money, or, simply, more money in or less money out. Value realization brings data monetization home. Realizing value from data is about converting value created—efficiency or customer value—into money or getting money directly from data by selling it. The ultimate goal of data monetization is bottom line improvement—reducing costs or growing earnings. Staying focused on realizing value increases the odds that your data investments will pay off and that the organization will not leave money on the table. So, even though this book is mainly about how to create value, the imperative to realize any value you create should always be kept in mind.

Questions to ask yourself

How does your organization create value using data today? How well does your organization report on the financial returns that result from these value-creating efforts? Can you track how much money data contributes to your organization's bottom line?

Research to consider

High-performing organizations—in terms of profitability, revenue growth, innovation, and agility—report that data monetization accounts for 10 percent more of their overall revenues than it does at their low-performing peers.[5]

Creating Value from Data

Over the past several decades, organizations have learned a lot about creating value from data. But arguably, the most important lesson is that creating value from data requires that a person or a system take some action it otherwise would not have taken. Data needs to be used to change the way something is done or to produce something new. Better processes and products create new value, not the data itself. This understanding is core to the data value-creation process, commonly referred to as *data-insight-action*. During this process, data is used by people (or systems) to produce an insight, the insight informs an action, and the action results in a valuable outcome. As figure 1.1 illustrates, data, insight, and action must all happen before value creation can occur: to grow valuable fruit, a fruit tree needs adequate soil and nutrients, the right amount of sun, and careful watering. If the data value-creation process breaks down or stalls—maybe there's a well-planted seed but no light or no water—then the associated investments in that little plant are merely sunk costs. This idea that the complete data-insight-action process precedes the creation of value is a fundamental data monetization idea that you may have encountered at a data-related conference, course, or event. It's a central idea in this book.

The data value-creation process (a.k.a. the data-insight-action process) *occurs when people or systems use data to develop insights that inform action, which generates value.*

Figure 1.1
The data value-creation process (a.k.a. the data-insight-action process)

Realizing Value from Data

Creating value from data is necessary but not sufficient. The final step is making sure that whatever value is created—something better, something new—contributes to the organization's bottom line. In other words, the "value created" needs to be turned into money. This step is value realization. Unless financial value is realized, data has not been monetized and the organization is now more costly.

Value realization *occurs when value that has been created from data is turned into money.*

Think about it. Fruit doesn't pick itself; when fruit stays on the tree, it is neither eaten nor sold. As figure 1.2 illustrates, the whole point of cultivating a fruit tree is for someone or some people to enjoy its fruits.

Value can be realized in one step or two steps. In the one-step process, data is exchanged for money in some form, and the money you

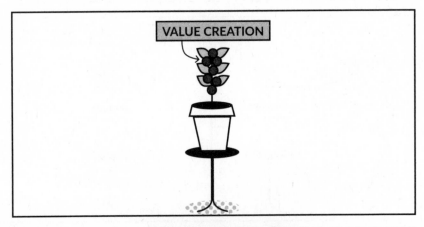

Figure 1.2
Value realization

receive for the data you sell is real and ready to count. Imagine an information business such as Nielsen selling consumer behavior data to a television network. Nielsen sets a price for the data; the network pays it. The data's value is realized with the sales transaction.

Value realization is a two-step process if it entails first creating something that has inherent value and then, second, cashing in that value so that it becomes financial value. The first step of creating value is the result of a data monetization initiative, but the second step, value realization, may require the involvement of multiple stakeholders. Step two could be the responsibility of a senior manager or leader if it requires higher levels of authority. For example, say a recruiting team uses data to make the new hire process more efficient. That's step one, and the efficiencies are inherently valuable. The crucial second step occurs when the efficiency gets turned into money by, say, cutting headcount and reducing the budget for onboarding new hires. When organizations have more resources than they need to sustain routine operations, that's referred to as "slack." Thus, in the second step, the slack created by the new, more efficient process is removed, making the organization better off financially.

Maybe a different data monetization initiative delivers a product enhancement that customers value. In that case, the second step requires that the product owner increase the product's price to reflect its higher value, allowing additional revenues to flow to the income statement.

The second step, realizing value, is often the tricky one. Cutting budgets and repricing products is not something that just anyone can do. Suppose the organization is not pushing to cut expenses or is reluctant to increase prices. In that case, it might be easier for a process owner to just let slack be absorbed by employees or for a product owner to let the value of product improvements go home with customers. It might even be desirable to do so in some circumstances. But if the slack that arises from a data monetization initiative isn't removed or if the additional value of a product is not extracted from customers, the data monetization initiative will not contribute to the organization's bottom line.[6] The initiative cannot claim to have monetized data.

IMPROVING   WRAPPING   SELLING

Figure 1.3
Three approaches to data monetization

Three Approaches to Data Monetization

There are three distinct approaches that organizations can use to monetize data, as shown in figure 1.3.

Improving uses data to create efficiencies in work from better, cheaper, or faster operations. Realizing value requires removing or redirecting the slack created by the efficiencies that, ideally, flow to the organization's bottom line.

Wrapping uses data to enhance products such that customers want to buy more or are willing to pay more. Value realization requires raising prices or selling more of the products to improve the bottom line.

Selling is the exchange of an information solution for some form of money. In this way, realizing value is straightforward and appears in the form of new financial inflows.

Research to consider

In 2018, 315 executives were asked whether their organizations were creating value via improving, wrapping, or selling. Across the sample, 50 percent strongly agreed that they were creating value from improving, 33 percent strongly agreed they were creating value from wrapping, but only 19 percent strongly agreed they were creating value from selling.[7]

Improving

Improving is the most common way that organizations monetize data, and examples abound. The United Parcel Service (UPS) used vehicle route data to optimize delivery routes to save US$400 million annually.[8] Columbia Sportswear used historical package-tracking data to eliminate root cause issues in their supply chain. This decreased both out-of-stock and overstocking problems, saving more than US$27 million in inventory costs.[9] Trinity Health used data from smart hospital beds to speed up nurse response time by 57 percent. Leaders at Trinity Health associated the nurse response time improvement with a reduction in patient falls, likely decreasing the cost of patient care.[10]

> *Improving is a data monetization approach that generates money when organizations use data to change the economics of work for the better and then remove or redirect the resulting slack.*

Most organizations have experience using data to improve business processes and work tasks. Many were inspired by the Business Process Reengineering (BPR) movement in the 1990s that encouraged organizations to analyze and design efficient workflows and business processes.[11] To execute BPR, organizations applied technology to clean data and boost its availability. The data was then used to analyze the root cause of process slowdowns, to measure the benefits of moving from an old way of work to a new, more radical way, and to monitor and manage critical process metrics. The BPR movement convinced many organizations of the benefits of data-driven process or task improvements. But a negative result of this movement was that many organizations got in the habit of assuming that the benefits of process improvement would make their way to their bottom lines. In fact, it takes organizational attention, resources, and discipline for financial value to materialize from efforts like those at UPS, Columbia Sportswear, and Trinity Health.

Quantifying the outcome from improving takes two steps. First, organizations need to measure the uplift in efficiencies or quality that result from improving with data. Second, they must remove or redirect the slack created by those efficiencies or productivity improvements. Some complications make the value of efficiencies hard to turn into money: sometimes, an improvement in one process creates efficiencies in downstream processes; or slack created by an improvement is used to relieve overworked or stressed employees; or efficiencies gained in a process show up in increased production or reduced inventory rather than slack. But if an improvement is supposed to reduce costs or budgets and they don't change, data is not being monetized.

Wrapping

The second data monetization approach is wrapping. Wrapping initiatives create data-fueled features and experiences to increase the customer value proposition of a product. When we say "product" in this book, we're referring to the thing an organization delivers to a customer that satisfies their needs. This might be a good or a service, it might be virtual or physical, or some combination of all of these. We use the terms "product" and "offering" to refer to whatever is delivered to the customer.[12] To realize some of the value created by an enhanced product, the organization must raise the product's price or sell more of it. "Selling more of it" could mean selling more units of the same offering to an existing customer, selling more related offerings, selling to additional customers, or sustaining sales of a product whose sales are eroding.

> Wrapping *is a data monetization approach that generates money when organizations use data-fueled features or experiences to enhance the value proposition of a product and then raise prices or sell more products.*

Opportunities to wrap products are everywhere; look around at the surge in connected devices and the new personalized ways organizations engage with customers. Some examples of wrapping include adding information to offerings in the form of reports, alerts, scores, visualizations, or dashboards that complement or enhance the offering and make it more appealing to customers.

The wrapping approach to data monetization can create distinctive offerings in the marketplace. Consider Schindler, an elevator maker. The company complements its elevators with an equipment performance dashboard to help building managers monitor elevator performance. Intergovernmental organizations like the World Bank provide portals for contributing governments to show them that their donations are achieving their desired philanthropic goals. Healthcare insurers add visualizations for health plan administrators to help manage their healthcare costs. In each case, an offering—an elevator, a philanthropic initiative, an insurance plan—is wrapped with data, insights, or action to make them even more attractive to customers (or other constituents).

Any offering can be wrapped, even diapers![13] Pampers is one of several diaper companies that developed sensors to attach to diapers that send a mobile alert via an app to parents when the diaper is wet. The app also tracks information about the baby's sleep and wake times. It's hard to imagine a product that could not be wrapped.

In the digital era, organizations are expected to wrap their offerings using data-fueled features and experiences that delight customers. But too often, they assume that they are realizing value from those efforts—without verifying whether and how much money hits their books. As it does with improving, data monetization by wrapping takes organizational attention, resources, and discipline. It requires that organizations first gauge the extent to which customers regard the product more positively because of the wrap. For example, do customer loyalty scores go up? Do customers recommend the product more enthusiastically? Second, organizations need to cash in on this positive regard by extracting revenues from customers, for instance, by raising the price of the offering.

There are also complications with data monetization by wrapping: sometimes an enhanced offering has already been paid for, and the opportunity to raise prices will only arise in the future. Sometimes wrapping staves off competitive pressure on prices or increases switching costs, thus retaining customers who might otherwise have been lost. In those cases, there might not be an immediate lift in sales but instead a future lift in sales or dampened sales erosion. However, none of these complications are reasons to ignore the step of value realization. Wrapping must make financial sense, or the associated investments might have been made more profitably elsewhere.

Selling

Companies have been monetizing data by selling information for decades. Consider the retail industry: retailers have sold their point-of-sale (POS) transaction data to companies like IRI since the late 1970s.[14] IRI, in turn, sold aggregated data and analytics back to retailers (and other organizations) that wanted to better understand their product sales compared to those of their competitors.[15] POS data is an important raw material for the aggregator because they can generate a substantial revenue stream from it.

> Selling *is a data monetization approach that generates new revenues when organizations commercialize data in the form of an information solution.*

Instead of purchasing reports or metrics from the aggregators, some retailers exchanged their POS data for these solutions. This is bartering, which is a financial transaction. In fact, both retailers and aggregators must regularly assess whether the tender they receive for their POS data and analytic reports justifies the expense or risk of the exchange.

This book will refer to a data product as an "information solution" to distinguish it from other kinds of products. Information solutions are standalone offerings that solve compelling customer problems. Customers might buy an information solution because it includes scarce data that they need, because it will help them get their own products to market faster, because of its sophisticated algorithms, or because the interface is user-friendly, to name just a few reasons. A subscription to Bloomberg news, data, and trading tools is an example of an information solution. Another example is IBM's Weather Company data application programming interfaces (APIs), which serve climate, environment and forecast data from a cloud-based platform.[16] Note that selling is one of three approaches to data monetization, yet too many organizations may naively view selling their data as the only way to monetize it. When organizations limit what they view as a data monetization opportunity, they end up leaving money on the table. A lot of money.

The Improve-Wrap-Sell Framework

All three data monetization approaches—improving, wrapping, and selling—are distinct ways of turning data into money. Their differences are summarized in table 1.1. Together, the three approaches make up the improve-wrap-sell framework. Regardless of industry, business model, size, geographic location, or strategic intent, your organization can monetize data using some combination of improving, wrapping, and selling. In chapter 7, you will read about how to choose what combination of approaches is right for your organization.

Because of the distinctions in how initiatives create value, they require different capabilities, demand different owners, entail distinct risks, and call for unique metrics and measurement methods. This will be covered in detail in chapters 3, 4, and 5. In brief, the success of improving depends on the leadership of process owners who define needed changes, recognize the opportunity for applying data, and ensure the adoption of changes. Wrapping demands engaged product owners who can envision the value offered by data to their products. They must be willing to engage with other parts of the company—like IT and customer service—in ways that were not necessary when developing and selling the core product. Finally, selling requires the identification of an

Table 1.1
Three approaches to data monetization

	Improving	Wrapping	Selling
Value-creation process	Data creates efficiencies (and thus slack) by making operational processes or tasks better, faster, and cheaper.	Data enhances the customer value proposition of products.	Data is commercialized and sold in the form of information solutions.
Value-realization process	Slack is eliminated or redirected.	Customers pay more or buy more.	New revenue streams are generated.
Measure value realization via	Impact on the bottom line		
Who is accountable for outcomes	Process owner	Product owner	Information solution owner
Key risks	Lack of action taking and value creation	Negative impact on customer value proposition when a wrap falls short	Inability to create or sustain competitive advantage

Source: Barbara H. Wixom and Jeanne W. Ross, "Profiting from the Data Deluge," MIT Sloan Center for Information Systems Research, Research Briefing, vol. XV, no. 12, December 17, 2015, https://cisr.mit.edu/publication/2015_1201_DataDeluge _WixomRoss (accessed January 10, 2023).

entrepreneurial leader who can envision and launch a new information solution for new customers.

Similarly, the three approaches entail distinctly different risks. The risk with improving is that the data-insight-action process will break down and value will not be created. Process owners are ideally suited to manage this risk by carefully tracking likely value creation and making course corrections. The risk associated with wrapping is already familiar to product owners: that the product enhancement adversely affects the value the customer enjoys from the core offering. Product owners, fortunately, already know how to track customer satisfaction;

they will need to follow similar protocols when implementing wraps. Finally, the risk associated with selling is the risk that accompanies any new business venture: business failure due to the inability to create or sustain competitive advantage. Information solution owners must remain highly sensitive to competitive pressures from substitutes and new entrants.

A Final Appeal for the Term *Monetization*

All organizations should make sure their data investments pay off. And today, data investments can be enormous. Data investments could simply make the organization more costly to run if no one is making sure that value is being created and realized. As a basic business principle, organizations should generate more money from their data assets than they invest in producing and managing them. If you buy into the concept of data monetization but simply don't like the term data monetization, you are not alone. It's distasteful for some. Some organizations, especially noncommercial ones, have little appetite for the term. This likely comes from leaders associating data monetization with going too far with data, with unacceptable exploitation of data assets, or with data trickery or sneaky tactics.

If you really can't bring yourself to use the term right now, call it what you want. Just make sure you use a term that links data to your organization's bottom line. It helps to have clear, shared language that people can use in discourse and debate. If everybody in your organization uses the term data monetization to mean the same thing, you should be able to have fewer discussions about whether it's ethical to monetize data and more discussions about how to monetize data ethically.

Time to Reflect

The status quo in most organizations is a flurry of data activity but no coherent vision of what it means to monetize data. Here are the key points from this chapter to keep in mind:

- As shown in figure 1.2, the fruit (the value) emerges at the end of the value-creation process. *What kind of value do your data initiatives most frequently create? How well are you measuring data-fueled value creation today?*

- Assuming a data initiative creates some value (there is fruit on the tree), that value should be realized (the fruit should be taken off the tree) by moving it to the firm's bottom line. *Do you just assume that value is realized from your data initiatives, or do you know it made it to your bottom line?*

- There are three basic ways to monetize data: using it to improve work, using it to wrap goods and services ("products"), or selling an information solution to someone else. *Can you think of an opportunity to use each one of these approaches in your organization?*

- Improving, wrapping, and selling initiatives should not all be managed the same way. *Who owns your different improving, wrapping, and selling initiatives? They're not all owned by IT, are they?*

- Organizations should generate bottom-line impact from their investments in data. *How comfortable is everybody in your organization with using the term data monetization to describe this?*

Data monetization is an incredible opportunity for organizations. But it's not simple. For one, it requires specific capabilities that help organizations create widely accessible data assets. In the next chapter, you will read about those capabilities.

2 Data Monetization Capabilities

In many companies, any business unit has the autonomy to hire a firm to [help them] grab data, toss it in a data store of their choice, and slap an individual use case on top of it. This happens over and over and over. It takes a different mindset and approach to build capabilities for consistency across a variety of use cases.

—Brandon Hootman, Caterpillar, Inc.

Why can some organizations monetize their data again and again, while others have hit-or-miss results? An organization that consistently monetizes data is leveraging some robust enterprise data monetization capabilities. This chapter covers how to build the five capabilities that produce data assets that are accurate, available, combinable, relevant, and secure. Data assets with these characteristics are easily reused, and reusable data assets lead to faster and cheaper data monetization initiatives. Organizations recognized for excellence in data monetization don't just engage their advanced capabilities. They also prioritize making it easy for people throughout the organization to access each capability.

Generally speaking, capabilities are the ability to do something. Capabilities can exist at a foundational level or they can be advanced. For example, most home cooks can boil an egg for breakfast; a professional chef can take an egg and turn it into something unexpectedly delicious. A diner may have line cooks on staff who consistently prepare a limited set of menu items, whereas a restaurant known to have an advanced cooking capability likely has a chef and supporting staff who can create a variety of sophisticated dishes. The ability to cook at an advanced level is usually acquired through education and experience, and it no doubt has an element of talent to it.

In organizations, it's common to bring people specializing in a particular capability (e.g., accountants) together. Not only do they learn from each other as they work together, but everybody in the organization also knows where to find that capability (in accounting). If the ability to do something is only needed in select parts of the organization, then the organization simply needs to establish a *local capability*. For example, a global company needs local experts in tax law in each country in which it operates. They are highly valued in their geography, but their expertise doesn't need to be available to other countries.

When a capability is applicable across the organization, it should be an *enterprise capability*. For example, an enterprise "digital asset management" capability allows communications teams worldwide to pull official brand images from a centralized system. Producing, approving, and organizing such media content only has to happen once; the images can then be used and reused in various sales and marketing contexts.

Questions to ask yourself

Can your organization turn data into accurate, available, combinable, relevant, and secure assets that people can reuse? Or are there skills and knowledge that are obviously missing?

Research to consider

Organizations who are top performers in data monetization outcomes have capabilities that are about 1.5 times stronger than those of bottom performers, and the top performers' outcomes are 2.5 times better than the bottom performers.[1]

The Five Data Monetization Capabilities

Data monetization capabilities are a collection of material resources and abilities or proficiencies that organizations rely on to develop their data into reusable data assets. A couple of decades ago, we studied information businesses like Nielsen and IRI, which rely on data assets for their economic survival, to understand their business models. It turned out that the key to these information businesses was that they had five advanced data monetization capabilities.[2] As the research moved on to investigating data monetization in other kinds of organizations, it became clear that these five capabilities are key to any data monetization initiative at any organization. Yes, any organization—including yours—needs data management, data platform, data science, customer understanding, and acceptable data use capabilities.

Figure 2.1 shows the five distinct data monetization capabilities laid out in the shape of a fan. The five capabilities work together. While these capabilities may not surprise you, they certainly are not easy for organizations to master.

Here are descriptions of the five capabilities and what it means to achieve an advanced level of each one. Later in the chapter, you will read about capability building at the financial services company BBVA.

Data management A data management capability is the ability to produce data assets that people can find, use, and trust. Organizations with advanced data management capabilities can report on the accuracy of their data, match related data entries, consolidate and streamline data fields, and integrate related data from external sources, such as data aggregators and suppliers.

Data platform A data platform capability is the ability to capture, transform, and disseminate data assets securely and efficiently. It leverages contemporary, cloud-based software to ingest, process, secure, integrate, and deliver data assets. Organizations with advanced data platform capabilities can cost-effectively distribute data assets inside and outside the organization at scale.

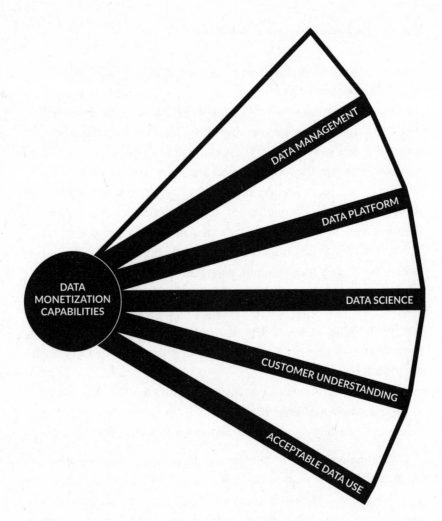

Figure 2.1
Five data monetization capabilities

Data science   A data science capability is the ability to use scientific methods, processes, algorithms, and statistics to extract meaning and insights from data assets. Organizations with advanced data science capabilities support data-savvy people across the organization in making evidence-based decisions. They leverage advanced statistics and techniques such as machine learning to inform and automate processes and products.

Customer understanding   A customer understanding capability is the ability to gather accurate and actionable knowledge about customer needs and behaviors. Organizations with advanced customer understanding capabilities accurately grasp what customers need and value, can cocreate with customers, and can formulate and test hypotheses about customer preferences.

Acceptable data use   An acceptable data use capability is an organization's ability to gather, store, and use data assets in ways that are compliant with existing laws and regulations and consistent with organizational and stakeholder values. Organizations with advanced acceptable data use capabilities have contextualized norms and policies. They have scalable oversight processes, which ensure that employees, partners, and customers appropriately engage with organizational data assets.

Capabilities are, by nature, fairly abstract. To make them less ambiguous, let's look at the specific practices that build up each capability.

Data Monetization Capabilities Accumulate from the Practices You Adopt

Data monetization capabilities come mainly through learning by doing, and so they are shaped by the practices you adopt. For example, when an organization adopts a foundational practice such as customer journey mapping, it gradually builds foundational data monetization capabilities, such as the ability to gather knowledge about customer needs (customer understanding). Once foundational practices are well established, more complex practices can be adopted, leading to more

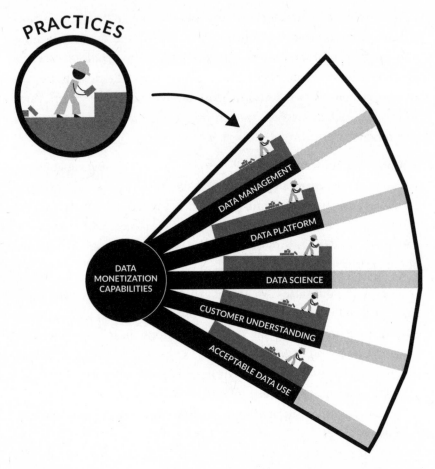

Figure 2.2
How organizations use practices to build capabilities

learning and higher-level capabilities. As a result, as illustrated in figure 2.2, as people and systems undertake more and more complex data monetization practices, their capabilities get more robust, and the fan becomes fully built out to its edges. Your organization will progress from foundational to intermediate to advanced capability levels as it adopts increasingly sophisticated capability-building practices.[3] There's no shortcut to acquiring robust data monetization capabilities; they are the result of steady work in the right direction.

Take the data science capability as an example: Typically, organizations first become proficient at basic reporting dashboards and visualization. Next, they master statistical techniques and approaches. Then they learn how to use machine learning and specialized analytics like natural language processing. It's nearly impossible to fast-track a data science capability by pumping money into machine learning tools (an advanced practice). At best, that would yield a pocket of underused machine learning tools that most of the organization simply would be unable to exploit. An organization needs to walk before it can run. People need to learn (and apply what they are learning) as they progress from foundational to medium to advanced practices.

The next section identifies practices that organizations adopt to build and invigorate each data monetization capability.[4] Practices come in many different forms. They may be expressed as policies ("Cloud first!") and backed up with procedures for minimizing deviations from the policy. They may be automated (programs for managing access to data), embedded in tools (statistical packages or AI modeling tools), or expressed as rules and routines (how customer feedback will be aggregated and shared). As you will see, there are three levels of practice that have been associated with building three levels of capability. There are no doubt other practices that can substitute and achieve similar capability-building outcomes, but research has validated the practices listed below.

Data management   To build a data management capability, organizations engage in practices that turn data into accurate, integrated, and curated data assets.

- *Master data (foundational):* Practices that produce reusable data assets include establishing automated data-quality processes, identifying data sources and flows that describe core business activities or key entities like customer and product, creating standard definitions of priority organizational data fields, and establishing metadata for those data fields.
- *Integrated data (intermediate):* Practices that allow data to be integrated from both internal and external sources include mapping and

harmonizing data sources and standardizing, matching, and joining data fields.

- *Curated data (advanced):* Organizations use taxonomy and ontology to curate their data. These practices involve analyzing data and its relationships, depicting data and its relationships in a way that is accessible and meaningful to users, and maintaining that depiction over time. These practices make it possible to augment the organization's data assets with data assets from external sources or with data assets created as a byproduct of the development of AI models.[5]

Data platform To build a data platform capability, organizations engage in practices that allow them to draw on cloud, open source, and advanced database technologies to produce software and hardware configurations that satisfy their data processing, management, and delivery needs.

- *Advanced tech (foundational):* The adoption of cloud-native technologies is an example of a data platform practice. Modern database management tools include products that leverage leading-edge techniques for data compression, storage, optimization, and movement.
- *Internal access (intermediate):* The use of APIs to offer data and analytics services internally is a practice that eases access to raw data or data assets from any system.
- *External access (advanced):* APIs can also be used to make an organization's raw data or data assets available to external channels, partners, and customers. Providing APIs to stakeholders outside the organization requires adopting practices for certifying external users and tracking their platform activity.

To give you a sense of what it looks like to engage in these data management and data platform practices, consider Fidelity Investments, a Boston-based financial services company. In 2019, the company kicked off a multiyear effort to rationalize one-hundred-plus data warehouses and analytics stores into a common analytics platform.[6] Fidelity invested in data management practices such as creating a common identifier for each major data entity at the company, for example, customer, employee, and investible security. It adopted practices for creating definitions of more than three thousand company data elements and building a central taxonomy and catalog to organize this new company terminology. Fidelity's data platform practices included installing a new modern, cloud-based analytics platform to house, process, and serve up the company's data assets to people across Fidelity.

Data science To build a data science capability, organizations engage in practices that advance their ability to use data science techniques and thinking. They hire new talent and upskill and develop existing employees. They invest in tools and methods that support data science work so that data science tasks can be appropriately managed and scaled.

- *Reporting (foundational):* Practices that foster the use of dashboards and reporting include standardizing data presentation tools and designating which data assets will be regarded as the "single source of truth" for process outcomes or business results. They include educating employees about data storytelling and evidence-based decision-making.

- *Statistics (intermediate):* Practices that promote the use of math and statistics include selecting analytics tools, hiring people with sophisticated mathematical and statistical knowledge, and establishing data science support units. They include teaching probability, statistics, and skills that increase the usability of analytics tools and techniques.

- *Machine learning (advanced):* To promote the use of advanced analytics techniques such as machine learning, natural language processing, or image processing, organizations engage in feature engineering, model training, and model management. They use AI explanation practices that ensure AI models are value generating, compliant, representative, and reliable.[7]

Customer understanding To build a customer understanding capability, organizations connect with customers to collect data about them—demographics, sentiments, context, usage, and desires—from which they extract analytical insights about core and latent customer needs.

- *Sensemaking (foundational):* Listening to customers and making sense of their needs is an example of a foundational customer understanding practice. Customer-facing employees can help organizations identify important customer needs by sharing ideas via "suggestion boxes" or crowd-sourced innovation events. These employees can also participate in agile or cross-functional teams tasked with mapping customer journeys or designing new products and processes.

- *Cocreation (intermediate):* Engaging customers in the cocreation of new products or new processes requires practices for identifying the appropriate customer, establishing the terms of customer engagement, and making good use of customer time.

- *Experimentation (advanced):* Common practices for testing ideas with customers include hypothesis testing (observing customer behavior to see if it conforms to expectations) and the use of A/B testing (using randomized experimentation with two variants, A and B).

Beginning in 2015, Australian insurer IAG made a significant investment in its data science and customer understanding capabilities when it acquired the forty-person customer insights company Ambiata.[8] In effect, IAG acquired experienced data scientists, who brought an influx of data science practices into the company—statistical techniques, machine learning, and analytics methodologies. A year later, in December 2016, IAG created a new division—Customer Labs—that merged experts in data, analytics, marketing, customer experience, design thinking, and product innovation. Customer Labs benefited from customer understanding practices that Ambiata had mastered during its years as a customer insights company, like A/B testing and experimentation.

It took several years for IAG to diffuse the Ambiata practices across the enterprise (so that many IAG employees could contribute to and use the advanced data science and customer understanding capabilities). The company actively drove diffusion by using its new Customer Labs division to test and refine Ambiata practices until they were a good fit for IAG.

Acceptable data use To build an acceptable data use capability, organizations engage in practices that allow them to effectively address regulatory and ethical concerns regarding data asset use by and about employees, partners, and customers. Organizations draw on this capability to mitigate the risk of using data assets inaccurately, undesirably, or in ways that are not contractually or legally allowable.

- *Internal oversight (foundational):* Practices that ensure acceptable use of data by employees usually begin with establishing data ownership; training employees about laws, regulations, and organizational policy; setting up data access approval processes; and auditing employee data access.

- *External oversight (intermediate):* Practices that ensure the appropriate use of data assets by partners begin with establishing clear agreements about appropriate use with partners and end with auditing partner use of data assets.

- *Automation (advanced):* Practices that allow customers to self-manage their data begin with establishing policies regarding customer control of data. These policies are then implemented both by communicating the policies to customers and facilitating customer control through automation. Automating practices also helps organizations scale internal and external oversight activities.

In 2019, Anthem Health added to its acceptable data use capability by hiring a technology and governance provider to stand up a cloud-based environment in which Anthem could collaborate with start-ups, academics, and others who wanted to use its deidentified patient health data set to develop and validate AI models.[9] There were big issues to resolve: data access, development standards, intellectual property rights, and more. The provider's technology allowed Anthem to set up base contracts with parameters that could be tweaked to accommodate the distinct needs of each partner's project; this made the up-front contracting process far more straightforward.

Figure 2.3 depicts the capabilities fan with advanced states in all five capabilities. When each capability is developed to around the same level, the fan could be said to be "well-rounded." Because the five data monetization capabilities are highly complementary, they should ideally be developed to similar levels of advancement. It will be difficult to fully exploit an advanced data platform without also having advanced data management and advanced data science capabilities in place. That said, the five capabilities rarely grow at the same pace. Sometimes an organization has developed one or two capabilities more fully than it has developed others, making for a lopsided and possibly ineffective fan. It is likely to be obvious where additional practices would strengthen the collective power of the five capabilities.

Assess Your Data Monetization Capabilities by Assessing Your Practices

While capabilities are very difficult to measure precisely, practices can be observed and assessed, and they are a good proxy for an organization's capabilities. Consider the earlier cooking example: it's almost impossible to look at two people and discern who is the amateur chef and who is the pro. But you can easily recognize an advanced cook by watching her behavior in the kitchen: how does she choose a knife, decide when meat is done, and plate the food? These are actual, observable practices that roll up to a credible evaluation of a person's cooking capability.

You can use the capability assessment worksheet in the appendix to evaluate your organization's data monetization practices. Follow the instructions to rate your practices and reveal your organization's capability levels.

Enterprise Capabilities Make Initiatives Faster and Cheaper

Your organization may have considered adopting some of the practices identified above for reasons of efficiency or cost without realizing their value in terms of advanced data monetization capabilities. Someone might push a practice (or policy or rule or process) for other reasons without realizing that the practice will help build a data monetization

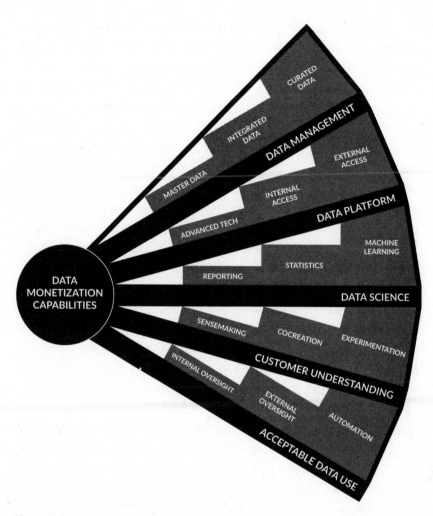

Figure 2.3
Advanced states of the five data monetization capabilities

capability. For example, an organization might adopt a "cloud first" policy for financial reasons without realizing that it is an important foundational practice for making data assets available for reuse both internally and externally.

Organizations must adopt practices at the enterprise level if they are going to build enterprise capabilities. Ideally, you want practices to strengthen capabilities into ones that can be repeatedly shared across the organization for use by any improving, wrapping, and selling initiative. Cloud-native applications, for example, let developers quickly create and deploy individual microservices without disrupting any other microservice; the developers' teammates can reuse what works. Adopting enterprise customer understanding practices ensures that customer insights gained in one part of the organization are captured and available to other areas. It can take some time and effort for organizations to migrate local data capabilities into an enterprise capability (consider how IAG slowly incorporated practices from its acquisition into the greater IAG company), never mind to grow new enterprise capabilities organically, from scratch. You can, however, imagine the payoff as capabilities build up and are available to be used pervasively and in new ways.

You can think about the value of enterprise capabilities within the context of racing. Imagine that you own a Formula One racing team. You would want to race your fancy car on some beautifully engineered track, with luxurious stands and amenities for spectators, shared and secure fueling, nicely fitted-out facilities for your pit crew (and your data scientists), and carefully engineered security barriers to protect your driver. You'd expect the race host to provide all those shared and reusable capabilities. Your time would be spent designing the perfect car, finding and motivating the best driver, and crafting a winning strategy.

In the best of all possible worlds, figure 2.4 shows what data monetization initiative teams want from their organizations: excellent data monetization capabilities—great data management to fuel the initiative, a great data platform for a fast and smooth ride, great data science

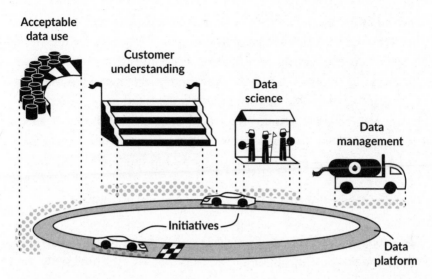

Figure 2.4
The great enterprise capabilities that teams want from their organizations

to optimize the initiative, great customer understanding to make sure customers are well served, and great acceptable data use to keep the initiative safely on course. When enterprise capabilities serve the needs of initiatives, those initiatives have a smoother, faster path. Teams are free to focus on the specifics of their initiative: managing stakeholders, developing the team, and training models.

Before your organization races ahead to build enterprise capabilities, it's important to note that capabilities only create value if they are used. In fact, organizations can't take too much time or spend too much money building enterprise capabilities before they start leveraging them. Enterprise capabilities that aren't used are just sunk costs. Nevertheless, an organization's long-term goal is the perfect, fully equipped racetrack—a set of advanced enterprise capabilities—that gets used over and over by many and varied initiatives.

The reality is that most practices are initially adopted by initiative teams, so most data monetization capabilities are developed in the context of initiatives. When enterprise capabilities do not exist, the initiative owner must unearth the capabilities needed to meet her objectives.

Her initiative team might try out a new tool, experiment with a cloud platform, or work out an acceptable use policy just because they need to conclude their particular initiative successfully. However, when an organization adopts the data monetization practices it needs initiative by initiative, it can end up with local capabilities that are hard to leverage elsewhere. It takes some vision and leadership to accumulate enterprise capabilities. This perspective may be found in the C-suite or a chief data office, where a top-down, global mindset is expected.

Building Enterprise Data Monetization Capabilities at BBVA

Let's look at an example of how one organization built its enterprise data monetization capabilities to advanced levels over time. BBVA has been recognized for excellence in generating data monetization outcomes and for having great data monetization capabilities.[10] It did not, however, begin its journey with its capabilities in an advanced state. In 2011, the 154-year-old financial services group was challenged with legacy technology that was costly and slow, employees with outdated data science skills, and heavy regulatory constraints regarding data use. Yet over time, because its leaders took a long-term perspective on capability building, the company established advanced enterprise data monetization capabilities that support all kinds of data monetization initiatives across its global presence.

Phase 1: Selling Initiatives

In 2011, BBVA leaders were curious about the viability of selling anonymized bank card data to generate new revenues. They sent a small team to the MIT Senseable City Lab to come up with information solutions that some market would want to buy. Leaders gave the team five million anonymized bank card records, which the team prepared for analysis. This meant adopting data management practices to clean up the data and to define fields. It also meant learning how to confirm that records couldn't be reidentified and establishing parameters regarding where and how they could sell the data legally.

At the time, the use of cloud computing at BBVA was banned by regulators. But while the innovation team was at MIT, it was free to use and learn about cloud software and services, so it did. It also learned how to use algorithms and visualization techniques that were far more advanced than anything that existed within the bank. The team's MIT experience made it realize that collaboration with others outside the bank could be very worthwhile. Learning how to collaborate with entities like start-ups, government agencies, and philanthropic organizations turned out to be key to developing meaningful prototypes, which the team then used to understand what kind of customers would be interested in bank card information solutions and how much those customers would be willing to pay for them.

After working with MIT for four years, the BBVA team had successfully completed several selling initiatives, validating that customers would pay for carefully analyzed bank card data assets. Also, it successfully established an initial set of new practices and capabilities that BBVA could leverage for future initiatives that involved selling bank card data offerings. It had learned how to identify promising markets that could benefit from economic impact analyses, such as urban planning and government agencies.

This effort convinced BBVA leaders that selling data was a viable strategy. At that point, the leaders set up a legally separate wholly owned subsidiary called BBVA Data & Analytics (D&A). The new entity was small, at first only four people, and was expected to become self-funding. D&A would do this by operating as a separate information business that sold information solutions based on the bank card data assets that had been produced during the years of innovating with MIT.

To reinforce D&A's autonomy, BBVA located the group in a building in Madrid separate from the bank. The new physical space was designed to include contemporary features that inspired collaboration and innovation (e.g., movable furniture, glass wall whiteboards). The physical separation from the incumbent bank helped preserve and nurture practices and lessons gained during the MIT experiences so that new capabilities could thrive.

As a separate information business, BBVA D&A could adopt practices they deemed worthwhile and build advanced enterprise capabilities required to sell bank card information solutions. It's important to note, though, that the unit was operating at a tiny scale. They offered a small set of solutions to some narrowly targeted markets, and the resulting revenues were minuscule compared to the revenues of the incumbent bank. D&A's small-scale adoption of advanced practices translated into incredibly advanced capabilities but for only a small set of data assets.

Phase 2: Improving Initiatives

As the BBVA D&A data scientists engaged in selling initiatives, they also networked with data colleagues in the larger parent bank over coffee and informal lunches. The subsidiary's data scientists began to realize that BBVA's internal data efforts could be more fruitful with the more advanced technology and practices they had adopted. As a result, they offered to help a few of their bank colleagues approach their initiatives differently. In one case, BBVA D&A used its more sophisticated data science capability to help an initiative more effectively optimize the placement of bank branch locations. The collaboration resulted in US$35 million in cost savings.

BBVA executives were thrilled to learn that data could create so much value by improving the bank's operations, but they realized that the bank needed capabilities supporting different data assets, not the ones the subsidiary had to offer. In effect, the bank needed capabilities like the subsidiary but in service to other kinds of data. For example, bank functions needed data assets for credit risk, customers, website activity, and more, not just bank card transactions.

To generate more data assets that they could exploit, data scientists from the subsidiary began advising internal bank initiatives and teaching them how to use data science tools and techniques. The subsidiary still had to fund itself, so it hired a financial expert to make sure every initiative it advised had a stated economic goal and a way to measure its level of achievement. If returns were positive, the subsidiary pocketed some of the returns, per its consulting arrangement with the bank. The subsidiary also absorbed 10–20 percent of the initiative's costs under the condition that the initiative contribute to the build out of the bank's enterprise capabilities. So, improvement initiative by improvement initiative, the subsidiary helped the bank accumulate data assets and algorithms, and they pitched the new data assets and algorithms to new initiatives to encourage reuse.

BBVA's IT group agreed to support the centralized platform over time, adopting more modern practices for its operation and its oversight. By 2017, the subsidiary had helped the bank deploy more than 40 improving initiatives for 27 different business units. As a part of those initiatives, the subsidiary helped unlock 34 new data assets by migrating 188 associated data tables to a cloud-based enterprise platform that future initiatives could leverage (thanks to a new cloud policy). Notably, BBVA D&A tracked capability building as a part of its performance management process. For example, it tracked how many new assets areas the D&A collaborations helped to unlock for BBVA as well as other metrics like the number of reusable machine learning models and the number of BBVA data miners who had been upskilled to become data scientists.

Phase 3: Wrapping Initiatives

The BBVA D&A data scientists next realized that they could contribute to the bank's digital presence by using some of their algorithms and ways of working to create appealing features for several of the bank's consumer-banking products. It was a hard sell, at first, to convince BBVA leaders to invest in using data science to enhance the customer experience because the business case was not like that for an improving or selling initiative. So, the D&A team offered to pilot a single feature, a spend categorizer that would use analytics to organize a customer's transactions and then present the results in a pie chart. It helped customers understand how they spent their money. Unfortunately, the initiative took longer than expected. For one thing, the customer data, a data set they had not previously dealt with, needed to be cleaned up and made perfectly accurate. To put it another way, it needed to be turned into a data asset. Also, the D&A team had to learn how to build and train from scratch an AI model that could categorize customer transactions.

The spend categorization had to be easily understood by BBVA's customers; otherwise the feature could do more harm than good. So, the initiative team learned how to experiment with A/B testing to establish a mechanism for understanding, over time, how well the feature was meeting customer needs. Soon after BBVA launched the categorizer, it became one of the most popular parts of the bank's digital experience, second only to money transfers. The resulting feature helped earn BBVA recognition for best mobile banking in 2017, and the bank won that award for many years after.

Building Capabilities Means Constantly Adopting New Practices

When BBVA transitioned from selling to improving, it discovered that its enterprise data monetization capabilities fell short. Its data assets were insufficient, the company's platform could not handle broad internal access, and local data science skills were outdated. This shortfall happened again when BBVA introduced wrapping; employees, it turned out, didn't truly understand customers because they were using outdated perspectives and techniques. To some extent, these shortfalls occur because improving, wrapping, and selling data monetization approaches rely on different capability profiles.[11] Improving, wrapping, and selling each place unique demands on an organization. For example, organizations focused on improving business processes will need internally focused capabilities, like a searchable catalog of shared data terms and definitions for employees to use to find data assets that can be used for analyses about operations. Organizations focused on wrapping offerings or serving new customers in totally new ways will need to focus on governance policies and processes regarding how employees can and should use customer data assets. Chapters 3, 4, and 5 will explore the capability profiles for improving, wrapping, and selling in detail.

Time to Reflect

Here are the key points from this chapter to keep in mind:

- Capabilities are built by adopting practices. *Consider your organization's weakest capability: What practices does your organization need to adopt?*

- Capabilities are often built to serve the needs of a particular initiative. *Consider your organization's most robust capability: How was it built or acquired? What practices contributed the most to its current state? (If you don't know, is there someone in your organization who could tell you?)*

- Enterprise capabilities are more valuable than pockets of capabilities all over the organization. *Which of your capabilities is the most "enterprise," that is, widely shared? How did it become an enterprise capability? What tactics have been used to prevent initiative teams from building isolated capability silos that are of limited, local value?*

- Capabilities only create value if they are put to use. *What policies, habits, or norms do you have in place that will ensure that the initiatives that are underway find and use capabilities?*

- Capabilities produce data assets that are accurate, available, combinable, relevant, and secure. Data assets with these characteristics are easily reused, and reusable data assets lead to faster and cheaper data monetization initiatives. *Does your organization make a distinction between data and data assets?*

The nice thing about getting a handle on your capabilities is that you can spend more time thinking about ways to exploit them! That's coming next. In the upcoming chapters, you will learn how you can become great at improving, wrapping, and selling.

3 Improving with Data

We will gain great efficiencies in the way we operate by having data and technology help make faster and more informed decisions.
—Robert Phillips, CarMax

Your organization likely has been improving with data for decades. But even if it's commonplace for you, you might not be going about it systematically or strategically. An organization with a state-of-the-art improving approach can be recognized by (1) its vision for improving, (2) the amount of value it creates and realizes, (3) the state of its capabilities, and (4) who is held responsible for improving initiatives.

Does your organization have a specific vision for improving with data? Do leaders encourage employees to be "data driven" and stop there? Or, instead, do they encourage the use of data "to move from worst to first" (in some respected industry-specific ranking), "make every employee one hundred times faster," or "eliminate one hundred million hours of wasted customer time"—or some other compelling goal? Imagine how much easier it is for employees to use data productively when they know what to aim for and what will be rewarded!

How well are you creating and realizing value from improving initiatives? With improving, the value-creation process is under the organization's control (unlike wrapping and selling, where customers are involved). This means the organization can—at least in theory—directly and actively manage the organizational adjustments needed to ensure that value is both created and realized.

How strong are your data monetization capabilities? Do analysts take personal pride in handcrafting byzantine spreadsheets and pivot tables? Do data miners use software introduced in the age of data warehousing (or earlier!)? Is data stored hither, thither, and yon? If that feels familiar, it likely means that your organization needs to update its data monetization capability-building practices. As you read in the last chapter, any data monetization approach—including improving—benefits from better enterprise data monetization capabilities. Better capabilities, better outcomes.

Who is responsible for your improving initiatives? Is it the "IT department"? This chapter will persuade you that the responsibility for improving initiatives, the value they create, the value you realize from them, and the capabilities you build for them must be shared among a much larger crowd of stakeholders.

Questions to ask yourself

As you read this chapter, think about an expensive, inefficient, or ineffective work practice at your organization. Maybe it's hard to onboard a customer or respond to supply chain glitches. Can you fix that problem using data? Do you know how you would measure and monitor the value created and realized from improving that work practice?

Research to consider

Among MIT CISR survey respondents, improving accounted for 51 percent of their financial returns from data monetization initiatives, making it the most prevalent of the three approaches in the improve-wrap-sell framework.[1] This likely reflects the maturity of improving in the marketplace.

Types of Improvements

Most organizations invest in improving initiatives. In a 2019 study of AI initiatives,[2] forty of the fifty-two initiatives studied targeted improving a process or a task,[3] ranging from predicting equipment failure to forecasting passenger demand to recognizing abnormalities in lab images. For example, GE created an AI-based contractor assessment for its three thousand Environment, Health, and Safety professionals that assessed whether a contractor satisfied GE's safety criteria. This improvement saved hours of time during contractor onboarding. (To give you a sense of the scale of this improvement, at the time of the research, GE was hiring approximately eighty thousand contractors annually.)

All improvements focus on enabling one of the three steps of the value-creation process that you read about in chapter 1: they offer data (*data improvements*), offer insight (*insight improvements*), or take some action that creates value (*action improvements*). The names indicate the scope of the improvement. As figure 3.1 illustrates, a data improvement, which just provides data, relies on the recipient to grasp the significance of the data, take some action based on that understanding, and create value. An insight improvement offers task guidance, but the recipient must then act based on the guidance to create value. With action improvements, the organization is sure to create the value it set out to produce because the action is taken (or nearly so) by the initiative.

Improving by Offering Data

Many improving initiatives provide more accurate, timelier, or better integrated data to a user who previously did not have access to that data or spent a great deal of time cobbling data together from various sources into a spreadsheet. One of the supposed benefits of business intelligence reporting initiatives was that they delivered much better data up and down the organization. But was that data used productively? Did users know what to do with it? In a few cases, yes; in many cases, no.

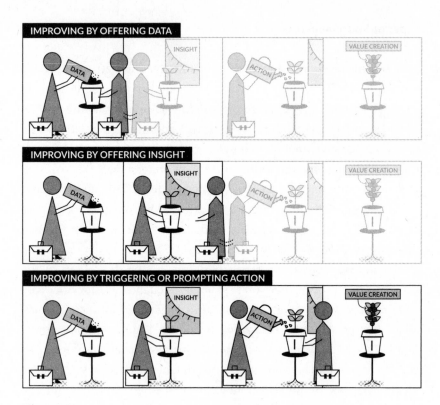

Figure 3.1
How improvements differ in their scope

Sometimes an improving initiative does deliver high-quality data to decision makers who know what to do with it and are motivated to act. Many will remember that the US Securities and Exchange Commission (SEC) failed to detect the Bernie Madoff Ponzi scheme for so long in part because the numerous tips that citizens submitted went to so many different people that no one recognized a pattern of concerns.[4] To protect against similar mistakes in the future, the SEC created a single data repository (TCR) that consolidated tips, complaints, and referrals. This far superior data source was put into the hands of analysts capable of using it to identify potential violations of securities laws. Once the analysts surfaced a possible violation, they were responsible for setting the wheels in motion for further investigation, which resulted in either

TCR resolution or enforcement action (i.e., creating value from the TCR data). The key was getting the right data into the right hands.

But more often, an organization has to do much more than deliver high-quality data to smart decision makers. Organizations also must actively ensure people can and are willing to engage with that data. Users cannot engage when they are poorly trained. (Data literacy programs and analytics training are great ways to address such skill hurdles.) Also, users will not engage when they are distrustful or too busy. If you choose just to offer data, make sure you monitor that data's use as well as the steps between use, value creation, and value realization.

Improving by Offering Insight

Improving initiatives can offer insights in the form of benchmark scores, exception reports, advice, and different kinds of visualizations and alerts. While offering insight in no way guarantees the use of insight, it is at least one step closer to value creation.

At contemporary apparel retailer GUESS, the data science team won over the company's creative staff (clothing buyers and designers who had little time or inclination to embrace insights based on data) by giving them cool devices, hiring a graphic artist to develop a fun, contemporary app experience, and creating visual dashboards that included photos of apparel and store layouts.[5] As a result, the buyers and designers began using insights about top-selling fashions, regional demand, and effective merchandising. They saved time previously wasted in making sense of tabular reports with cryptic SKU numbers because everybody was "already on the same page" regarding important product sales trends. Based on the accessible and consumable insights, they focused their time on developing and deploying new selling, demand management, and merchandising strategies (i.e., taking actions that created value).

As a rule, insights are most likely to lead to action taking and value creation if they are delivered to people responsible for acting. Most of the forty AI initiatives mentioned earlier delivered insights to experts of some sort. For example, equipment failure predictions went to individuals responsible for taking equipment offline, not to a machine operator; passenger demand forecasts went to people responsible for changing flight schedules, not to caterers; alerts about abnormalities in lab images went to radiologists, not nurses. Insights must be delivered to people (or systems) who have the authority and ability to act on them.

Improving by Triggering or Prompting Action

As you might suspect by now, you can avoid the risk of a breakdown in the value-creation process by triggering or prompting action. Many AI-based improving initiatives trigger the automatic execution of some tasks. In the study mentioned earlier, one-third of the AI improvements involved automation. They included action taking like automatically remediating network security breaks, automatically reordering items that were low in stock, adjusting equipment settings after changes in the operating environment, and automatically sending an email containing ideal marketing content to a customer.

Full automation is not always easy to achieve because so many complementary organizational adjustments need to happen. Consider the case of Trinity Health, one of the largest healthcare delivery systems in the US.[6] An upcoming remodel for a flagship hospital provided an opportunity to pilot and execute IoT-enabled use cases, including one that helped nurses respond faster to patients and reduce patient fall risk. The improving initiative automatically sent an alert to a nurse's mobile device if a patient with a high risk of falling started to get out of a sensor-laden bed so the nurse could respond faster. Before the alert could be automated, the team had to do many things: establish business rules that spelled out exactly who to alert, in what order, and under what conditions; clean up the patient data and create accurate fall risk scores; redesign the process by which nurses made rounds; educate staff to follow the new processes and procedures; and create incentives that would get staff to buy into the new policies and procedures. After the initiative was deployed, Trinity leaders viewed this use case as a success. They created value in the form of a 57 percent reduction in nurse-call response time, which correlated with fewer patient falls.

In some initiatives, triggering or prompting action does not mean completely automating it but just making human action simple and straightforward. For GE's AI-based contractor evaluations, for example, a professional pressed a button to initiate evaluation assistance. The AI model then analyzed the document and reported on whether the GE safety criteria were satisfied or not. The application offered easy access to the rationale underlying the AI assessment, which allowed the professional to quickly accept most of the assessments and move on, creating significant efficiencies in the process.

Creating Value from Improving

When it comes to creating value from improving, initiative teams must first articulate the type and magnitude of value that the initiative intends to create. Then, they must make any complementary organizational changes that are needed to ensure that value gets created.

In a sea of possible improving outcomes, organizations must clarify up front what kind of value they most want to generate from an initiative. At times, initiative teams aren't sure if the type and magnitude of desired value is possible. In these cases, they draw heavily on pilot testing and experimentation. They can zero in on an initiative's value potential by investigating an improvement at a small scope or in a controlled manner. Pilot tests allow the organization to establish value baselines (e.g., the pre-improvement level of productivity of a process). Experiments often require developing a measurement approach for tracking value creation that, fortunately, can be sustained after deployment and over time.

For example, leaders at Trinity Health also wanted to know up front what kinds of value they could create from improving initiatives (like the nurse response initiative) in a "smart" hospital room. Specifically, they wanted to improve the quality and efficiency of patient care. But in what ways? The leaders asked a pilot team to fit thirty patient rooms with sensors everywhere: in medical devices, beds, patient wearables, and strategic locations like doorways and handwashing stations. In one pilot, the team tested whether monitoring hand hygiene would lead to better infection control outcomes (improving by offering data). Data from handwashing sensors and staff-location sensors was used to monitor handwashing as care providers entered a hospital room. Analysts then calculated handwashing percentages and correlated those with hospital-borne infection rates.

These results were shared with managers who were responsible for staff handwashing practices. The pilot test results justified broader deployment of the hand hygiene initiative and helped the initiative team establish realistic value-creation goals. Three years after the pilot, Trinity Health had recorded over 14.5 million hand washes, representing increased adherence to hand hygiene procedures within medical-surgical and critical care patient areas. This adherence had led to a 29.7 percent reduction in C. difficile infections and a 24.5 percent reduction in MRSA infections.

Regardless of whether an organization deploys an improving initiative that offers data or insight or triggers or prompts action, the complete data-insight-action value-creation process must happen for value to materialize. The top risk to value creation with the improving approach is not making it to action. One way to mitigate this risk is to extend the initiative's scope (as in figure 3.1). For example, once the SEC had its TCR database in place, it could streamline the work of analysts by providing them with actionable insights. That is, the initiative team would increase the scope of the improvement from offering data to offering insight. And at GE, until their contractor evaluation application served up easily accessed, clear explanations for the AI model's assessment, evaluators were more likely to ignore it and instead perform slow, manual evaluations. The GE initiative team increased the scope of the improvement from offering insights to prompting action.

Because so many inaction-risk challenges can pop up, it is important to be keenly aware of how the value-creation process is expected to unfold. If possible, the process should be monitored by either instrumenting data or insights to see if they are used or by asking users directly about use, periodically. Are there obstacles related to the ability of decision makers to use data that could be resolved with training or assistance? If insights are not being acted on, perhaps the insight is going to the wrong person, not someone with the authority and ability to act on it. As you saw with some of the improving examples, to make sure that an improving initiative creates value, it might be necessary to change related policies or business rules, redesign processes, change how data is collected, redesign jobs, change performance measures or incentives, and reskill or replace people.

Realizing Value from Improving

You already know from chapter 1 that organizations must stay on top of value realization from any initiative. And you know that improving initiatives often seek to standardize or simplify processes and work tasks, creating value in the form of efficiencies. For the organization to realize value from efficiencies, the resulting slack must be redirected or removed. That is, if the efficiencies reduce the need for headcount, the equivalent headcount must be removed from the process or redirected to other work. The savings flow to the bottom line. At GE, for example, the AI improvement initiative reduced the time GE professionals spent reviewing documents in the office, freeing them up to focus on higher-value work, like getting into the field to look for and solve safety problems. However, keep in mind that some slack is a good thing. Slack allows for innovation and also helps organizations deal with environmental uncertainties, such as sudden increases in demand.[7]

What was not mentioned in chapter 1 is that an improving initiative can also create value by making a process more productive or by improving product quality. The value created by producing more and better products is realized—turned into money—by selling them. Or, as in the case of GUESS and the insights for clothing buyers and designers, the value created in the form of better product placement was realized in the form of increased revenues from fewer discounts and markdowns. In other cases, realizing value from better products might require price increases. In chapter 4, you will read more about realizing

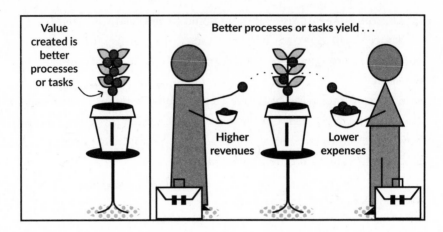

Figure 3.2
Value realization from improving initiatives

value from product sales, since that is the dominant value-realization mechanism for wrapping initiatives.

To summarize, as shown in figure 3.2, some of the value created by the improving initiative is realized by the organization as reduced costs, and some is realized by the organization as increased revenues. And some value is left on the tree, so to speak—some value has been created that is not turned into money. It might take the form of slack capacity to be used for innovation, it might reduce pressure on employees or managers, or it might go home with customers. The amount of value left on the tree could be considerable if slack is not removed or redirected.

Improving at Microsoft

Microsoft, one of the world's most recognizable technology companies, exemplifies a company that invested big in improving, with initiatives of all shapes and sizes. Though headquartered in the US, in 2022, the company operated globally, employing more than 163,000 people. Despite ongoing economic shocks and changes in consumer behavior, by June 2022, Microsoft had grown to a market capitalization value exceeding US$2 trillion.[8]

In 2014, the company faced increasing competition from the likes of Google, Apple, and Oracle as well as significant shifts in consumer behavior and expectations. In particular, the software industry's movement to cloud-based services called for a substantial change to Microsoft's business model: offering cloud services required constant information about service usage, a deep understanding of customer attitudes and needs, and entirely new pricing and selling strategies.

Incoming CEO Satya Nadella embraced this challenge in 2014 with outstanding results. Just three years later, cloud revenues had grown by 93 percent, and Microsoft's share price had more than doubled. Also, 61 percent of Microsoft employees were using data and analytics monthly. Nadella's clear vision, combined with the continued prioritization of evidence-based decision-making, resulted in a cascade of internal improvements that transformed Microsoft into a data-fueled organization.

Microsoft engaged in improving with an explicit vision. Like many CEOs, Satya Nadella used the term "data-driven" a lot as he talked with audiences both inside and outside the company. But it was obvious what Nadella meant by the term. He meant he wanted Microsoft employees everywhere, around the globe, to use data to change the very nature of their work so that the company could successfully transition from a software product company into a cloud-based services provider.

To back up his words, Nadella made bold moves. He consolidated core business functions (e.g., sales, marketing), breaking down product-oriented silos. He adjusted employee incentives so that one of the three core pillars of assessing an employee's performance was how well they collaborated across the organization. And he set a goal that every Microsoft employee would use Power BI to perform work. Collectively, these efforts created an environment in which leaders could create value from data. As a result, improving initiatives sprang up across Microsoft.

Let's look at one example of an improving initiative championed by leaders in finance (specifically one that offered insights). The leaders wished to raise the effectiveness of Microsoft's financial analysts by reducing the cycle time between financial analysis and field action.

The goal of the initiative was for analysts to spend less time analyzing financial data and more time communicating insights to their partners in sales. The finance team adopted a suite of comprehensive, flexible analytical tools so that analysts could answer a wide range of questions on the fly during business reviews and answer impromptu questions from sales personnel. To hone the analysts' communication skills and presentation techniques, leaders established a storytelling training program for them that included webinars, live demonstrations, videos, and in-person sessions. Within fifteen months, these efforts helped financial analysts reduce their time to produce insights by 30 percent and to redirect that time to sales partner communication. These outcomes aligned with Microsoft's need to create entirely new pricing and selling strategies as it shifted to its cloud services business model.

This short example demonstrates some key points about the improving approach to data monetization:

- Nadella's vision to shift to cloud services demanded significant efficiencies that would allow effort to be redirected toward sales.
- The example initiative made Microsoft's existing financial analysts more efficient by decreasing the time required to produce financial analyses.
- Analysts were also made more effective in that they could deliver more meaningful insights and immediately respond to their sales partners' queries.
- Finance leaders (i.e., the owners of the business process being improved) were accountable for ensuring value creation and value realization.
- To support the value-creation process (i.e., increase the likelihood that salespeople would act on the analysts' insights), finance leaders established a storytelling training program that taught analysts how to present actionable insights in a compelling manner.
- Finance leaders measured success (i.e., value creation) as the reduction in data-gathering time and corresponding increases in time devoted to sales partner communication.

- Value realization occurred when the time saved by analysts was redirected to the more valuable activity of supporting their sales partners who were growing sales.

Again, this is just one example of improving at Microsoft after Nadella came on board as CEO. There were many other new improving initiatives throughout the company.

Data Monetization Capabilities for Improving

Chapter 2 explained that five data monetization capabilities, namely data management, data platform, data science, customer understanding, and acceptable data use, power data monetization initiatives. Like any kind of initiative, improving initiatives with access to more advanced capabilities are associated with greater data monetization returns.[9]

If you are curious to know how advanced capabilities need to be, research indicates that organizations classified as top performers in improving (those that reported top scores in improving outcomes) have the distinct pattern of capability practices illustrated by figure 3.3.[10] (As you will see in the next two chapters, top-performing wrapping and selling organizations have their own distinctive patterns.)

While the organizations identified as top performers in improving have better capabilities than bottom performers (whose fans would be blank), they do not necessarily have advanced data monetization capabilities. They do, however, possess the following capabilities, which foster their ability to achieve their improvement goals:

- These organizations have accurate master data, particularly about operations, such as the chart of accounts, product or part numbers, employee identifiers, location codes, or asset identifiers.
- They provide internal access to data and tools through a data platform built using cloud and advanced technology, making data access fast, ubiquitous, and cost efficient.
- Their data science capabilities are well established at the statistics level, allowing them to provide insights necessary to optimize processes and tasks.

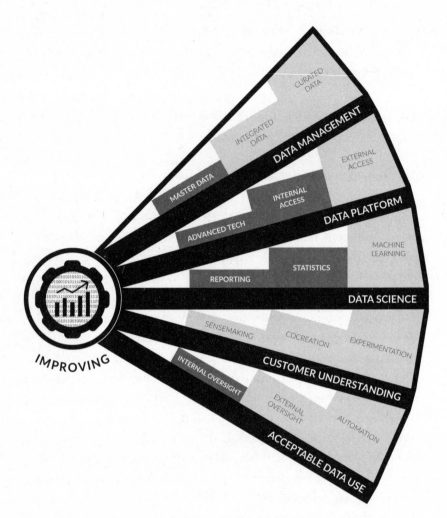

Figure 3.3
The capabilities of top-performing improving organizations

- A basic level of customer understanding is undoubtedly important for improving initiatives so that changes are made in line with customer needs. However, on average, top-performing improving organizations do not have a notable level of this capability. This is probably because many improving initiatives are not customer facing.
- Internal use of sensitive proprietary data is formally monitored and governed to ensure appropriate data use.

In sum, top-performing improvers draw on capabilities that help them produce data assets that can be reused in ways important for them.

Data Monetization Capabilities at Microsoft

People often assume that technology companies are great with data. But just like any organization, technology companies can establish capabilities locally instead of establishing data monetization capabilities at the enterprise level. They can also become comfortable with established ways of working with data—using spreadsheets and SQL queries—at the expense of introducing new tools and training.

This was certainly the case at Microsoft before Nadella's appointment. However, as Microsoft leaders and employees came to rely more on data, chief information officer (CIO) Jim DuBois established four corporate shared services groups to amass enterprise data monetization capabilities. These corporate groups worked closely with leaders across the organization to establish practices needed by new data monetization initiatives.

To illustrate the interplay between capabilities and initiatives, consider another improving initiative, one that streamlined Microsoft's sales processes. Sales leaders set out to increase the time salespeople spent with customers by 30 percent, or 1.5 more days per week. This goal was again driven by Microsoft's business model shift, which required salespeople to understand customer attitudes and needs more deeply.

Microsoft initially lacked the necessary *data management capability* for this initiative; critical data was buried in siloed, product-line applications, with inconsistent data definitions and coding conventions. Salespeople drew on data from more than eighty different systems.

They had to contend with multiple definitions of the term "sales lead," forcing them to waste time manually translating and integrating the information they needed. As a first step to a better data management capability, sales leaders adopted a process for standardizing shared sales concepts—such as what is meant by "pipeline" or "lead"—so they could build consensus on the agreed-upon definitions among salespeople, sales managers, and IT.

To provide salespeople around the globe with access to the new and improved sales data, Microsoft had to modernize its *data platform capability*. The company invested a year in developing the Microsoft Sales Experience platform using Microsoft Azure cloud technology. The platform team identified the key source systems from which to pull data and established data movement processes; standardized fields so that sources using different field identifiers and formats could be integrated; and established reference data (such as a standard list of country codes) to maintain consistency in the values of commonly used fields. The resulting platform ingested and consolidated sales data to produce 360-degree views of Microsoft's relationships with corporate customers. For each customer, this new system summarized purchases, issues and complaints, and previous communications.

The platform hosted a collection of dashboards driven by Power BI (Microsoft's own business analytics service) and other data services. Process designers arranged these dashboards into workflows to support different sales personas, such as sellers and sales managers. Each unique workflow offered users helpful access to the company's *data science capability*; the salespeople accessed information and actionable insights that were specific to their accounts and work tasks.

Because this initiative involved improving key customer-facing processes, a *customer understanding capability* was needed. (The earlier Microsoft example of improving the efficiency of financial analysts did not depend on a customer understanding capability.) They adopted a practice of drawing on the collective knowledge of the sales force, a foundational practice called sensemaking, or listening to customers and making sense of their needs. Salespeople provided input into workflow ideas, reporting requirements, and even features that could be used to feed sales-related machine learning models (e.g., a model to predict the likelihood of a deal closing). Their input, which in effect was infused into new work tools and tasks, helped Microsoft build a customer understanding capability.

Finally, Microsoft developed its *acceptable data use capability* by monitoring dashboard usage and being transparent about this oversight. The company remedied barriers to data access and curbed inappropriate use by providing better support, training, and incentives.

Microsoft's data monetization capabilities turned Microsoft's sales data into data assets reused by the reengineered enterprise sales process (an improving initiative that prompted salesperson action). To track value creation, sales leaders monitored their employees' use of dashboards and measured the decrease in time spent on administrative duties. To realize value, leaders encouraged salespeople to reallocate their time (on average, 1.5 days per week) to customer-facing activities. In effect, from this improving initiative, sales leaders realized value equivalent to avoiding the cost of increasing the size of their trained and experienced salesforce by 30 percent.

Ownership of Improving Initiatives

The ideal leader for an improving initiative is the owner of the process, activity, or task being improved; for simplicity, let's refer to improving initiative owners as process owners. A person in this role is accountable to the organization's leaders for a process or task outcome that influences the organization's bottom line (e.g., the cost of making something, the speed at which something is made, and the quality at which something is delivered). She understands what makes her process tick, how process tasks are accomplished, and what information is relevant to the work being done. The process owner also understands how the performance of her process relates to or impacts the organization's key performance goals.

At Microsoft, the owner of the sales improvement initiative was the head of Microsoft's enterprise sales business unit (not someone in IT, on the process design team, or leading data). Only this person was in a position to ensure that the desired value was created (an average reduction of 1.5 hours per week of administrative work) and to manage the risk of inaction. The head of sales drew on his power, clout, and control over resources to keep the initiative moving along. And he was perfectly positioned to redirect any slack created as a result of the initiative to other sales unit needs, as he did.

There are cases in which process owners need help from other leaders to realize value from productivity or product quality gains or to realize value from efficiency gains that arise in downstream processes because of improvement to the processes they control. For example, the owner of Microsoft's financial analyst improvement initiative, the person in charge of financial analysts, had to work with another leader—who had oversight of field sales—to make sure that financial analysts' efficiencies ultimately translated into their sales partners' generating additional sales.

As you might sense, process owners—and other leaders on whom they rely—are vital for improving initiatives. But it takes a village for improvements to succeed. For example, at Microsoft, the entire global workforce was expected to engage in new ways of work and use data whenever possible for tasks of any kind. At Trinity Health, smart hospital room efforts unfolded with the help of IT people, data analysts, clinicians, and all levels of hospital staff. At GUESS, improvements to selling, demand management, and merchandising evolved through collaboration among app programmers, graphics designers, data teams, store employees, operations teams, and increasingly engaged buyers and designers. In fact, in the improving examples throughout the chapter, myriad people from all levels across the organization have been responsible for some facet of data monetization. Improving, as it turns out, is everybody's business.

Time to Reflect

Regardless of their size, organizations that wish to explore improving initiatives should begin by considering their vision for improving, the value they intend to create and realize, their capabilities, and whom they will involve in improving initiatives. Like Microsoft's Nadella, leaders must be clear about how data assets will be used to improve operations and generate value. Organizations must also understand what data monetization capabilities are required to support their improvement goals and how they will be developed. Finally, for any improving initiative, leaders must designate a process owner with accountability for the initiative's success, who will be expected to share responsibility broadly among the many people who need to be engaged.

Here are the key points from this chapter to keep in mind:

- Improving initiatives deliver (1) data or (2) insight to decision makers, or they prompt or trigger (3) action. *Which kind of improving initiative (data, insight, or action) is easiest for your organization?*

- Improving initiatives don't create value until some action takes place. *For your improving initiatives that deliver data or insight, how well is your organization tracking action and value creation?*

- It is crucial that value created be realized and reflected in your bottom line. *Does your organization realize value from its improving initiatives? Or is it leaving money on the table?*

- Improving initiatives draw on all five capabilities, not just data management. *Looking back, can you think of an initiative that failed because the capabilities it needed were not available? What capability-fostering practices did that initiative require?*

- Improving initiatives should be owned by people who can ensure that value is created. *Looking back, can you think of an improving initiative that did not create value because the wrong person owned it? Who should have owned that initiative?*

Ultimately, improving is a great place to start if your organization is just beginning its data monetization journey. For organizations that have mastered improving, the subject of the next chapter—wrapping—is a natural next step.

4 Wrapping with Data

Companies that create enhanced customer experiences using proprietary data will limit the threat of substitute products and thereby create sustainable margins.

—Gregg Jankowski, AlixPartners

The last chapter explained how you can use data to improve work practices so that your organization produces more or better output at less cost. As you were reading chapter 3, you were probably focusing inward, thinking about how your organization functions today. Now it's time to turn your attention outward, focusing on enhancing what your organization produces as perceived by your customers or constituents. Data wrapping is all about your customer or whomever your organization serves.

When you use data to create a feature or experience for a product with the implicit objective of delighting the customer, you've created a wrap. You aren't generating a standalone information solution; you're enhancing the value of an underlying offering. The product can be physical (a tractor), intangible (a bank account), service based (a taxi ride), noncommercial (tax servicing), or for profit (freight delivery). All of these products can be wrapped. For example, a tractor can be wrapped with a digital display that shows operational performance; a bank account can be wrapped with a chart that categorizes the account owner's spending; a taxi trip can be wrapped with a fare estimator; a tax form can be wrapped with prepopulated fields; and freight delivery can be wrapped with notifications of expected delivery times. These features and experiences offer exciting possibilities if your organization struggles with product commoditization and rising customer expectations. In a competitive environment, wrapping can help your offerings stand out in the marketplace.

Perhaps your organization feels pressure to give customers and stakeholders more. You might have efforts underway to map out customer journeys, find and fulfill unmet customer needs, or engage in customer cocreation. If you do, it's time to consider data wrapping and tap into a world of data-fueled ways to change or freshen up your offerings.

Questions to ask yourself

As you read this chapter, reflect on the friction your customers—or constituents—experience with your current offerings. How can you use data to make your products more useful, easier, or more fun to experience? Can your offerings do more to help your customer save money, make money, or achieve a goal that matters to them?

Research to consider

In 2018, of five-hundred-plus product owners surveyed, 85 percent had wrapping initiatives underway, and 55 percent of those wraps were already deployed in the marketplace.[1]

Types of Wraps

Organizations today must be able to walk in the shoes of their customers. This is true whether they are working hard to sell goods or services, to achieve a philanthropic mission, or to serve the needs of a constituency of citizens. Delivering effective and enjoyable offerings is only possible with a deep understanding of customer needs and the extent to which customers perceive those offerings are meeting their needs.

By listening to their customers, organizations might learn that their offerings are inconvenient to buy, cumbersome to use, or hard to return. Wraps to the rescue! Wraps can help customers at any point along the customer journey. Wraps that help a customer solve a problem related to the offering make the offering more valuable to the customer. Most websites and apps deliver wraps that enhance core offerings. Consider an app for a meal kit service that helps a customer choose suitable meal options, manage nutritional intake, and identify optimal recycling options. These informational enhancements are wraps that help the customer better acquire, use, and retire their meal kits.

Wrapping can add value to offerings in both business-to-consumer (B2C) and business-to-business (B2B) settings. For example, chapter 2 recounted how BBVA offered a spend categorizer to consumer-banking customers to delight them and get them to use their bank cards more often. The wrap used machine learning algorithms to sort customer transactions into rent, food, and other budget categories and then displayed a customer's spending activities as a simple chart. The bank promoted the categorizer as a way for BBVA consumer-banking customers to manage their financial health.

Later, BBVA also created wraps for business customers. The bank offered store activity dashboards to merchants that purchased BBVA POS services. This dashboard wrap drew on data collected, anonymized, and aggregated from BBVA bank card transactions and POS terminals. It displayed insights and alerts that answered common merchant questions like, "How much total revenue is my business generating compared to the average in my business sector?"

All wraps fall into one of the same three basic types that improvements did. They offer data to the customer (*data wraps*), offer insight to the customer (*insight wraps*), or take some action that benefits the customer (*action wraps*). With wraps, the customer achieves a goal by taking an action as a result of being presented with data, an insightful analysis, or an action trigger. And by taking action, customers create

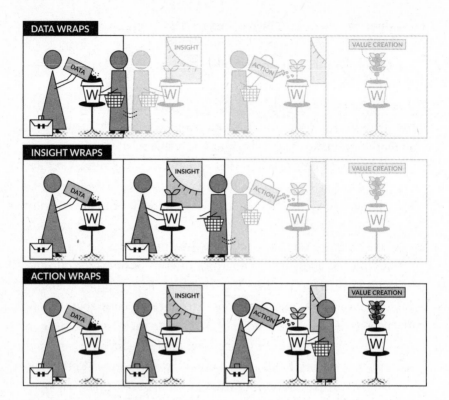

Figure 4.1
How wraps differ in their scope

value for themselves. Whether and how the organization realizes value from the wrap is a topic to be discussed later.

The names for data, insight, and action wraps simply describe the scope of the wrap in the value-creation process. A key difference in the three types of wraps is the organization's visibility into the customer's value-creation process. As figure 4.1 illustrates, the wrap that simply provides data leaves insight finding and action taking to the customer. The organization has little visibility into whether and how insight and action happen and how much value is created for the customer. An insight wrap points the customer in the right direction, but the customer must take the action that creates value. With action wraps, customer value creation is all but guaranteed because the wrap is designed to trigger action. Insight and action wraps can be instrumented to give the organization some visibility into use but not necessarily into value creation.

All of this should sound familiar to you—unless you skipped the last chapter. The important twist in this chapter is that wrapping is intended to help your customers achieve their goals, not to help you and your colleagues achieve your goals.

Data Wraps

Data wraps offer customers data that can take many forms: simple reports, dashboards, charts, and even data feeds that customers can integrate into their own systems. For example, social media companies give advertisers simple reports detailing how consumers are responding to their ads. Advertisers can use this information to review the success of their ads and withdraw, adjust, or expand their social media advertising buys. Some local governments give citizens simple reports that reflect a household's status with the municipality. Citizens can log in to a portal to assess their compliance with local obligations like dog licensing and their standing with local services like garbage pickup.

Compared to the other types of wraps, data wraps do the least work for the customer, so they have the weakest association with customer value creation.[2] That is, data wraps are the least likely to generate customer value. However, one attraction of data wraps is that they require the least effort to launch.

Insight Wraps

An insight wrap simplifies customer decision-making or problem-solving with respect to the core offering. Wraps that offer insights provide customers with the next steps to take, recommendations, flags for irregular activities or unusual data patterns, benchmarks, or alerts.

A food and beverage provider offered a party planner chatbot to party hosts to prevent over- or underspending on drink and snack purchases.[3] The chatbot used advanced analytics to analyze historical sales data and generate optimized shopping lists for the hosts based on the type of party and the number of attendees. Those party hosts who followed the recommendations created value for themselves by throwing a less costly party. It's worth noting that not all party hosts will do this! As an insight wrap, the chatbot relied on the host to follow through and make the recommended purchase. Some hosts might have second-guessed the list, restricted their purchases to items for which they had coupons, or ignored the list entirely. For all those party hosts, the chatbot would not have lived up to its value-creating potential.

Insight wraps get organizations one step closer to customer value creation than data wraps; they point customers to possible solutions that could generate value for them. However, for customer value to materialize, these wraps need to deliver insights that customers can understand and act upon to achieve their own goals. As a result, insight wraps require more advanced data monetization capabilities than data wraps, particularly more advanced data science skills and a deeper understanding of customer wants and needs.

Action Wraps

If the food and beverage provider's chatbot had ordered the items on the shopping list for the party host, then it would be an action wrap. It would be taking action on behalf of the party host. Imagine if the chatbot could detect the party host's current location, discover which stores in the area had the shopping list items in stock, order them, and schedule the order for drive-through pickup. Now that would be an action wrap!

Action wraps typically include analytics features that first determine what change in the customer's situation is needed. Then the wrap comes as close as possible to making that change happen. There are some interesting action wraps in IoT contexts. For example, one farm equipment provider placed sensors on its equipment and collected data to monitor performance (device status, temperature) after it was installed on the customer's premises. The equipment provider created an action wrap that predicted potential equipment failure, ordered parts, and scheduled a service call on behalf of the customer.

Sometimes action wraps require the customer to initiate the final action, but they make it very easy to do so. BBVA created an app feature that notified a customer about a refinancing opportunity that appeared to fit their needs. It offered to connect the customer with a live financial advisor who was teed up to support the customer with a refinancing option. The feature laid the groundwork, but the customer made the final move with a click.

So, if action wraps are so great, why don't organizations always create wraps that act? Well, often, they can't. They might not be confident what action should be taken or be allowed to act for regulatory reasons. They might also not have suitable systems or processes in place, or their customers might not want them to act. For these reasons and more, data and insight wraps might have to suffice. But regardless of the kind of wrap the organization creates, it's always important to keep the customer's final action (or actions) in mind. What will the customer do with the data or insight provided in the wrap? What kind of value—and how much value—will that action create for the customer? As you will see later, the amount of value the customer creates from the wrap puts a ceiling on the amount of money the organization can ultimately realize.

Characteristics of Great Wraps

Wraps that customers find useful and engaging are more likely to increase unit sales, command higher prices, grow market baskets, and improve customer retention.[4] Useful and engaging wraps have four characteristics: They *anticipate*, meaning the wrap understands the customer's need in advance. They *adapt*, meaning the wrap meets the customer's need in a tailored way. They *advise*, meaning the wrap supports evidence-based decision-making. And they *act*, meaning the wrap performs an action that benefits the customer. Figure 4.2 illustrates these four characteristics, called "the four As."

Let's take BBVA's spend-categorizer wrap as an example. In 2016, BBVA was first to market with its pie chart of categorized expenses, so it

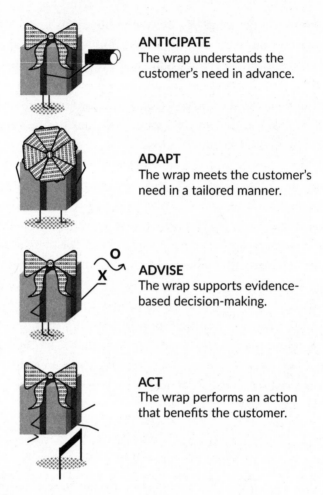

ANTICIPATE
The wrap understands the
customer's need in advance.

ADAPT
The wrap meets the customer's
need in a tailored manner.

ADVISE
The wrap supports evidence-
based decision-making.

ACT
The wrap performs an action
that benefits the customer.

Figure 4.2
The four characteristics of useful and engaging wraps

captivated customers with its novelty. But today, that original pie chart
would not get high marks on the four As. It would get low marks for
anticipate because it was inherently backward-looking; it simply showed
what a customer had already spent. The early pie chart was somewhat
adaptive in that it had a few tailoring features based on customer needs
or preferences. It would get low marks for *advice* because the pie chart

didn't help the customer decide what to do about the information. The pie chart would also get low marks for *act*; the pie chart certainly did not take any action on behalf of the customer.

Intuitively, an insight wrap should earn high scores on advising, and an action wrap, of course, should get high scores for acting. The spend categorizer is a classic example of a data wrap. Data wraps, by their nature, primarily rely on features that adapt. They draw on customer-specific data and generate information tailored to the customer at hand.

Higher scores on the four As will increase data monetization out-comes for customers (in value creation) and organizations (in value realization), so it's only natural for organizations to evolve data wraps into insight wraps and then into action wraps over time.

Anyone who looked at BBVA's financial manager app five years after launch would have appreciated how far its features had come since the early pie chart days: BBVA customers could view predicted expenditures for the upcoming two months so that bills or payments wouldn't catch them off guard; that would earn this wrap a high score for *anticipate*. Customers could set spending targets, and the app would help them stay under the targets by alerting them before they reached a cutoff level; that would earn a high score for *adapt*. Customers could see, on average, what people in their neighborhood—presumably, people like them—were spending on things like utilities and food, which could lead them to rethink their spending; that would earn a high score for *advise*. Finally, as described earlier. the app could alert the customer to a new refinancing opportunity, connecting the customer with a loan agent with the push of a button; that feature would earn this wrap a high score for *act*.

In sum, the four As are a checklist that helps gauge a wrap's poten-tial for creating customer value. Organizations can score a wrap on the four As to determine how useful and engaging a wrap is likely to be. By comparing the scores of various wrapping proposals, organizations can identify the opportunities that are most likely to inspire action, create customer value, and pay off for the organization.

Creating Value from Wrapping

Customers' willingness to pay for an offering will increase when they believe the wrap has made the offering more valuable—that is, it is easier and more enjoyable to find, acquire, use, store, maintain, or retire the offering. This is the metric to watch when wrapping: has an uplift in the value proposition of the offering been created? Uplift can be monitored using various techniques, like tracking customer usage, A/B testing, conducting controlled experiments, or surveys. With an enhanced value proposition, the organization can attract new customers or motivate existing customers to pay more, spend more, or stay longer.

The Joint Sphere

Consider that when an organization delivers a wrap, it only creates potential value for its customers. Ultimately, it is customers who create value for themselves by taking some action at the end of a value-creation process; the organization gains if and when it realizes a portion of this value, for example, by charging a higher price or by retaining the customer's business despite competition. Therefore, customer value creation must be the primary focus of organizations that pursue the wrapping approach.

By designing a wrap to give the customer either data, insight, or action, the organization, in effect, chooses how and how much it will help customer value materialize. Organizations that care deeply about creating customer value want to work closely with customers in the design and development of wraps. The area of joint involvement in wrap design and development is called the *joint sphere* (see figure 4.3).[5]

The size of the joint sphere (the overlapping ovals in figure 4.3) represents the extent to which the organization and customer share knowledge (and related resources) to achieve the customer's goals. Without any joint sphere, the organization is on its own to discover how to improve the customer's value proposition. And if the joint sphere is very small, the organization will likely be restricted to offering a data

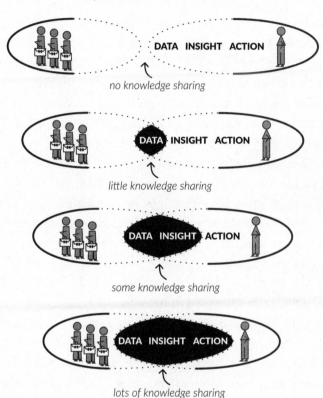

ORGANIZATION
participates in value creation

CUSTOMER
creates value

The more knowledge that an organization and customer share, the more an organization can influence customer value creation.

DATA INSIGHT ACTION

no knowledge sharing

DATA INSIGHT ACTION

little knowledge sharing

DATA INSIGHT ACTION

some knowledge sharing

DATA INSIGHT ACTION

lots of knowledge sharing

Figure 4.3

Organization and customer working together to generate customer value wrap. Conversely, when the joint sphere is large, the organization is more likely to have the opportunity to offer an action wrap.

A larger joint sphere results in better outcomes for customers and the organization alike. Customers are more likely to create value, and organizations are more likely to be able to realize part of that value for themselves. Organizations grow the joint sphere by building trust and digital connections with their customers. Customers grow the joint sphere by sharing their data and permitting organizations to take action on their behalf.[6] In B2B contexts, moving from transactional relationships to customer partnerships enlarges the joint sphere.

How can an organization expand the size of the joint sphere it shares with its customers? It can begin by discovering what customers are trying to achieve with its offerings—and how well (or not) those goals are being met. Initially, an organization can learn this information by asking customer-facing employees and by experimenting with data wraps that draw on the data it already has. Next, you will see how PepsiCo grew its joint sphere and changed the nature of its relationships with its large retailer customers.

Creating Value from Wrapping at PepsiCo

PepsiCo owns some of the world's biggest food and beverage brands, including Pepsi-Cola, Lay's, Gatorade, Tropicana, and Quaker. In 2021, PepsiCo's products were consumed upwards of one billion times per day in more than two hundred countries and territories, generating revenues of US$79 billion.[7]

Though the company had successfully established itself as a global leader in convenience foods and beverages in the late twentieth century, around 2010, PepsiCo saw industry growth begin to slow as markets reached maturity, competition increased, and its core consumer group aged. Rather than continuing to increase product variety, PepsiCo turned to data as a source of competitive advantage.[8] Specifically, the company wanted to use data to identify pockets of potential growth and understand when and where to place specific products in a particular retail outlet, among other goals.

In 2015, PepsiCo established a new business unit, the Demand Accelerator, that led the development of integrative, data-driven marketing services for its large retailer customers. The Demand Accelerator helped PepsiCo's IT unit build data monetization capabilities, provided enterprise-level analytics support, and supported new kinds of retailer collaborations. Ultimately, PepsiCo's collaborative approach to developing wraps helped build relationships that created win-win-win initiatives for shoppers, retailers, and the company itself. As a result, PepsiCo earned several industry awards recognizing its position as a top supplier.

The Demand Accelerator's collaborative approach played a key role in PepsiCo's wrapping efforts. One early example of PepsiCo's collaboration with retailers involved a convenience store and gas (C&G) retail chain that wanted to maximize its fountain drink sales, some of which were generated by PepsiCo's brands. However, the retailer did not have insight into drink sales because their scan data only reflected the purchase of a cup, not its contents.

The Demand Accelerator worked with the C&G retailer to solve this problem. First, they assembled PepsiCo's data about the number of gallons of syrup the retailer used. Together they combined that with the retailer's own data about its syrup purchases from other providers. Then, using advanced analytics, the Demand Accelerator identified specific store and shopper attributes that influenced syrup usage. Using data wrapping language, the Demand Accelerator created an insight wrap of analytics-based soda syrup usage influencers—things like a shopper's age and geography—to add value to its core offering of syrup. This insight wrap was made possible because PepsiCo's retailers trusted PepsiCo with their data and also trusted PepsiCo's analytics. Mutual trust is crucial to effective collaboration in the joint sphere.

The retailer acted on these insights, changing how it offered fountain drinks in a subset of its stores. The value the retailer created (for the retailer) by this action was evident in the increase in fountain drink sales that followed the change. Once the value of this change was clear, the retailer introduced the new tactic more broadly. PepsiCo did not directly charge the retailer for the Demand Accelerator services; instead, it realized value from the wrap (for PepsiCo) in the increased volume of the retailer's syrup purchases.

Over time, the Demand Accelerator played a significant role in supporting retailer partnerships. PepsiCo's relationships with its retailers were initially transactional, but those relationships evolved into collaborative customer partnerships due largely to the Demand Accelerator's activities. In effect, PepsiCo successfully enlarged its joint sphere with its retailers.

Realizing Value from Wrapping

It is sometimes straightforward to realize value from wrapping, as PepsiCo did when its retail customers bought more PepsiCo syrup. The realized value flows directly to the bottom line. As a rule, however, realizing value from wrapping requires understanding what kind of value and how much value customers create from your core offering because of the wrap. Based on this understanding, combined with knowledge of the customer, product owners can decide how to realize value: raising prices (to charge for the wrap), selling more of the product to existing customers, selling more complementary products, selling the product to new customers, or relying on the wrap to retain customers who might otherwise defect, as you read in chapter 1.

A wrap can also deliver internal efficiencies. For example, a side effect of a good wrap might be a reduction in calls to the customer service desk. Or an equipment wrap that preemptively schedules preventive maintenance might reduce the need for emergency service during off-hours. To realize value arising from the more efficient use of people or any other resource, someone needs to remove or redirect slack, just as they do with improvement initiatives, so that the savings can flow to the bottom line.

But there's a complication: these more efficient resources might not belong to the owner of the offering; they may belong to other functions and departments. So, getting those efficiencies to the bottom line will require cooperation from the heads of those units. Fortunately, some

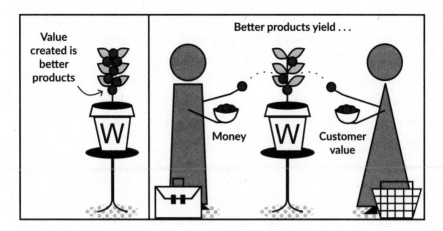

Figure 4.4
Value realization from wrapping initiatives

efficiencies (reduced inventories, reduced warranty costs) will flow automatically to the bottom line.

To summarize, as shown in figure 4.4, of the value created by the wrapping initiative, some might be realized for the organization as reduced costs or increased revenues—money—and some goes home with the customer. And some value is left on the tree, so to speak. That is, some value is created but not turned into money by the organization. Instead, that value might increase the organization's capacity for innovation, go home with employees and managers, or take the form of good customer relationships. The amount of fruit on the tree (the amount of value created) essentially sets an upper limit on how much value the organization can realize. In some B2B contexts, how much value the organization can realize is subject to negotiation with the customer.[9]

Measuring Realized Value for Wrapping

Organizations should know what value from wrapping is hitting their bottom line from additional sales and operating efficiencies so they can make sure they are investing in the right things. Nonfinancial value (employee satisfaction, customer loyalty, or extra time for innovation) should be measured as well. Some organizations have accepted methods for putting a value on their customer's loyalty or their brand capital. For example, at one time, Carlson Hospitality estimated that each new loyalty program enrollment added US$20 of value to its Radisson brand.[10] Ideally, a product owner will have recorded baseline metrics that can be tracked after the wrap is launched and going forward. This helps the product owner understand the impact of the wrap.

In the authors' research, product owners at a financial services company were great at measuring value from wrapping. For example, the product owner of one of the company's affinity credit cards prioritized wraps related to fraud reduction, which was a top concern for customers of that offering. Fraud reduction wraps for this card included digital transaction statements that contained merchant logos, geospatial maps that reduced the time and effort it took a customer to review their purchases, and email/text alerts when transactions suggested unusual activity, such as a tip amount that was disproportionate to the cost of a meal.

Across the financial services company, product owners monitored how customers reacted to new wraps by conducting experiments that compared the attitudes and behaviors of recipients of a new wrap to control groups of customers who did not receive it. The company's product owners always tied these customer reactions to changes in product sales. As a result, the product owner of the affinity credit card mentioned earlier could easily determine the extent to which a wrap feature increased usage of the credit card (and thus led to revenues).

The fraud reduction wraps were so intuitive and helpful to the affinity credit card customers that they led to a reduction in calls to the customer service center. Although the product owner did not plan for that value, the call center process owner gladly recognized the efficiencies and redirected the slack to cover other call center work.

In the public sector, tracing the value of a wrap to the bottom line can be challenging. For example, a wrapping initiative might get citizens to enroll in a public health program and save lives, reducing public health costs but in the long run, not the short run. At a philanthropic organization, a wrapping initiative might show progress toward

accomplishing key goals, leading patrons to donate more to that important cause. Or a government agency might need to wrap its offerings
just to keep up with citizen expectations of excellent service and to
avoid future taxpayer revolt. In even these cases, measurement is critical for understanding whether a wrap is doing its job. And when measurement can be used to report on success to key stakeholders, public
sector organizations can more easily increase or maintain their inflows
from donations, budget allocation, grants, and the like.

Data Monetization Capabilities from Wrapping

Organizations need to invest in data monetization capabilities to create
useful and engaging wraps (ones that earn high scores on the four As).
Suppose a product owner wants a wrap not just to anticipate and adapt
but also to advise and act. In that case, the organization will need more
accurate data, a faster platform, and deeper customer understanding.
Its acceptable data use capability might need to become more sophisticated, to include oversight of the use of data by algorithms and the
permissibility of acting on the customer's behalf.

Like the improving approach to data monetization, the wrapping
approach also requires all five data monetization capabilities described
in chapter 2. And, as with improving, wrapping generates greater
returns from more advanced capabilities.[11]

Research to consider

Product owners who say their organizations wrap more effectively than
peers reported an average return on investment (ROI) of 61 percent from
their wrapping initiatives, compared to just a 5 percent ROI by product
owners who say they wrap less effectively than peers.[12]

Organizations that are top performers in wrapping have better capabilities than bottom performers (whose fans would be blank). Still,

they do not necessarily have advanced data monetization capabilities, as shown in figure 4.5.[13] Organizations can achieve valuable wrapping outcomes without using machine learning or curated data for their wraps. Still, the kind of wrap matters: action wraps are difficult, if not impossible, to execute without advanced capabilities. Organizations do, however, need baseline capabilities that facilitate customer-savvy wrap development regardless of whether the wrap offers data, offers insight, or prompts action:[14]

- Top wrapping organizations draw on rich customer data assets regarding customer demographics, sentiments, relationships, core offering use, and interactions with the organization, integrated to produce a 360-degree customer view.

- By providing internal access to data and tools through a data platform built with advanced technology, they allow employees across the organization to access customer information.

- Their data science capabilities offer statistics skills and understanding, allowing them to provide insights to customers as well as to employees seeking to understand how well the organization is meeting customer needs.

- For top wrapping organizations, sensemaking, by listening to customers, is critical for surfacing not just core customer needs but also latent and unmet needs.

- All organizations that wish to pursue wrapping must have some acceptable data use capability in place to ensure that employees use customer data in compliant and ethical ways. However, the research indicates that this capability is difficult for organizations to build, and even top performers are still working to get the right new practices in place.

Data Monetization Capabilities at PepsiCo

The data monetization practices of PepsiCo's Demand Accelerator unit illustrate how much effort PepsiCo invested in capability building and how it has accumulated the enterprise capabilities required for wrapping initiatives. Even though PepsiCo had local data monetization

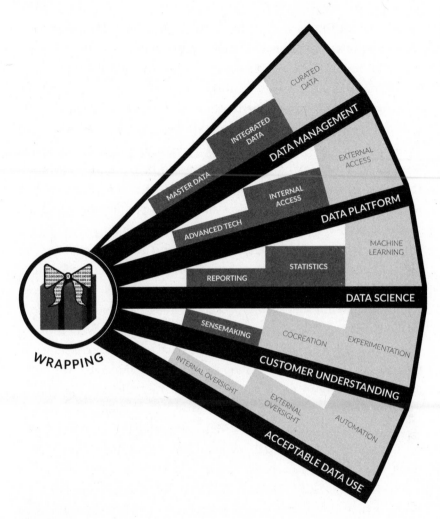

Figure 4.5

The capabilities of top-performing wrapping organizations

capabilities within each of its major divisions before 2015, they were siloed and often duplicated. As a result, different divisions were serving the same retailers in potentially inconsistent ways. The Demand Accelerator was set up to resolve this problem by centralizing and then diffusing enterprise data monetization capabilities across PepsiCo.

PepsiCo's capabilities grew from adopting practices like those used by top wrapping organizations. Back in 2012, the global IT unit had established a data taxonomy so that PepsiCo had a "single version of the truth" for its product sales, worldwide. The IT unit had also adopted master data management practices and housed product sales data in a single enterprise data warehouse. These practices built the company's *data management capability*. After the Demand Accelerator was established in 2015, its leaders worked with PepsiCo's global technology unit to build a data asset covering 110 million US households. This data asset was invaluable for identifying pockets of potential growth because it included not only consumers of PepsiCo products but most of the consumers in a given geographic region. The data asset about consumers—referred to as "Most Valuable Shopper" data—was integrated with data assets about PepsiCo product sales, further strengthening the company's data management capability. The Most Valuable Shopper data was carefully deidentified and structured to ensure that the data's use would be fully compliant with legal, regulatory, and ethical constraints. As a result, the company's *acceptable data use capability* grew stronger.

Together with IT, the Demand Accelerator established a cloud-based platform that allowed it to source and manage more extensive and more diverse kinds of data, drawn from both inside and outside PepsiCo. This platform was required to store, manage, and deliver the growing collection of data assets that fueled the Demand Accelerator initiatives. In addition, because it was API enabled and cloud based, it allowed secure access by retail partners, as needed. These practices contributed to the company's *data platform capability*.

The Demand Accelerator hired new expert data science talent and upskilled their own analysts to enhance the company's *data science capability*. The data scientists created easy-to-use dashboards and reports for marketing and sales employees across the organization. Engaging with and learning from these marketing and sales employees helped the Demand Accelerator better understand the needs of PepsiCo's retail customers. These practices helped strengthen the company's *customer understanding capability*.

Over time, people working in the Demand Accelerator packaged some of the customer-specific wraps they had developed (wraps similar to the earlier example of the fountain drink optimization insight wrap) into turnkey applications for other retailers. The applications supported common retailer use cases, like customizing the product assortment at a specific store based on the needs of its local shopper base and successfully launching and managing innovative marketing programs. As PepsiCo's data monetization capabilities became more advanced, the number of applications grew into a suite of wraps named "pepviz" that helped retailers optimize their store assortments and product sales.

Ownership of Wrapping Initiatives

The ideal owner for a wrapping initiative is the product owner. A person in this role is accountable to the organization's leaders for the overall success of an offering that the organization delivers to its customers or constituents. This product owner has deep knowledge of the strength and weaknesses of the offering's customer value proposition, how well the offering delivers on the value proposition in the view of customers or constituents, and how well the value proposition pays off in terms of financial returns to the organization. For this reason, the product owner should be accountable for a wrapping initiative regardless of whether the funding comes from the traditional IT portfolio funding process, the marketing budget, or elsewhere.

The product owner manages a wrap just as she manages any other product feature or experience. She needs to understand how the wrap is supposed to impact the product's customer value proposition. She weighs the costs, benefits, and risks of deploying the new wrap as part of the overall product management and development processes. She also prioritizes the wrap opportunity along with other product-related activities and investments.

At PepsiCo, the product owner for many Demand Accelerator initiatives was the customer account manager accountable for the profitability of the specific retailer or retailers who benefited from a particular wrap. So, for example, the owner of the fountain drink wrap was accountable for the C&G retailer account. That customer account manager was best positioned to understand how to formulate an appealing wrap, allocate budget and resources to make it happen, and identify what complementary adjustments would be needed to support this customer account and this wrap initiative. Without the account owner, the Demand Accelerator might have wasted a lot of company resources by developing a wrap that was unrealistic, undesired, or didn't pay off.

An important note is that the product owner is best positioned to mitigate the top risk associated with wrapping: value-loss risk. A wrap must meet service levels that are acceptable to the customer. The product's value proposition can deteriorate if the organization deploys a wrapping initiative that falls below the customer's expectations. Imagine a wrap that displays data that is wrong or takes several minutes to load! Product owners will insist that wrapping delight, not disappoint, their customers.

The product owner plays a vital role for data wrapping initiatives, but as with improving, wrapping requires getting all kinds of people on board to ensure success. Yes, wrapping, too, takes a village. Think of all the people who "touched" the fountain drink wrap at PepsiCo: data scientists and marketing specialists in the Demand Accelerator; data, systems, and technology people who worked with the data assets used for the initiative; sales teams; and people in supply chain and distribution who were needed to fulfill requests for more products. Indeed wrapping, like improving, is everybody's business.

Time to Reflect

Each touchpoint along the customer journey—at purchase, during use, or while engaging with customer service—offers different wrapping possibilities. And these possibilities might entail delivering data, insight, or action to your customers. Regardless of which wrap type makes sense for your organization and your offerings, you need to have a clear picture in mind of the customer's offering-related goals, how the wrap generates customer value, and how your organization can realize value. Here are the key points from this chapter to keep in mind:

- Wraps are enhancements to physical or intangible goods or services you offer to your customers. *Which of your offerings seems most likely to have a value proposition that could be enhanced with data or analytics?*

- Wraps can deliver data, insight, or action to your customers; action wraps require that you deeply understand your customers' value-creation process. *Where in your organization would you find that kind of knowledge of customers? Would you need to partner with customers to understand how they create value from your offerings and how that value could be increased?*

- Wraps differ in the extent to which they anticipate, adapt, advise, or act on behalf of customers. *Consider any wraps you already have for your offerings—how well do these wraps anticipate, adapt, advise, or act?*

- Wraps can create value for customers, and an organization can realize some of that value. *How do you realize value from your existing wraps? Do you have existing metrics or approaches to measure the value customers realize from your core offerings that you could exploit to assess customer value creation or realization from a wrap?*

- Wrapping initiatives draw on all five capabilities, not just customer understanding. *Looking back, can you think of a wrapping initiative that failed because the needed capabilities were unavailable? What capability-fostering practices did that initiative require?*

- Wrap initiatives should be owned by the owner of the offering that will be enhanced. *What will it take to engage owners of your offerings in a wrap initiative?*

In the process of wrapping some of your goods or services, it would not be unusual to get to know your customers well enough to see an opportunity to sell a customer (or a different customer) a completely new solution based solely on your organization's data assets. That's the subject of the next chapter.

5 Selling Information Solutions

First, you need to understand what your customer is challenged with. Then consider: what do you have that can be brought to the table to provide a solution and that can scale and grow in a changing environment?

—Don Stoller, Healthcare IQ

You've made it to the third approach to data monetization: selling information solutions. Before you picked up this book, there is a good chance you thought "data monetization" was just another name for selling data sets. Now you know that data monetization is much more than selling—it's improving and wrapping too! In this chapter, you will discover that selling involves more than selling data—it's selling insights and action too! Your organization can package and sell a variety of standalone informational solutions that help customers solve important problems.

Historically, organizations pursued selling when they recognized that they had data for which other organizations would pay handsomely. For example, in the medical supply distribution space, back in the 1990s, Owens and Minor (OM) accumulated loads of medical supply cost data as it distributed medical supplies from thousands of manufacturers to hundreds of hospitals. In 2004, it established a business called OM Solutions that converted OM's vast trove of cost data into data assets that that could be used to create hospital spend analytics solutions. The hospitals used the OM Solutions offerings to manage their medical supply costs more effectively and save money.[1] In the retail grocery space, Kroger established its 84.51° business to leverage POS data assets that were delivered to retailers via marketing analytics tools and advisory services. The retailers used the tools and services to create more personalized experiences for shoppers across their purchase journey and to make money.[2]

After learning about the challenges of the improving and wrapping approaches, it might seem simpler just to sell your organization's data to generate big returns. Warning: it's a rewarding but higher-risk option. The selling approach to data monetization involves standalone information solutions; there is no underlying core offering with a value proposition that is merely enhanced. Selling organizations must create information solutions with their own appealing value propositions for which customers would pay. They must create solutions that meet current market needs and then adapt and expand the solutions to continue to profit while serving new and changing market needs. And they must do this while fending off scrappy competitors eager to enter a potentially high-margin business.

Questions to ask yourself

As you read this chapter, imagine new opportunities for your organization. Are there problems that customers would pay you to solve? Can you fill that need by selling an information solution? Do you have data assets that could be used to inform such a solution?

Research to consider

Survey respondents, on average, reported that selling accounted for 18 percent of their revenues from data monetization activities, making it the least prevalent of the three approaches in the improve-wrap-sell framework.[3] No doubt, this reflects the complexities of selling information solutions.

Types of Information Solutions

As data proliferates, more organizations see opportunities to solve others' problems with their data assets. For example, a medical device manufacturer—with sensor data assets that reflected patient health—saw that it could help clinicians offer better diagnosis and care. A custodian bank—with actual cash flow data assets associated with private equity funds—saw that it could help investors evaluate and analyze private capital markets. And in chapter 2, you read that BBVA created a deidentified bank card data asset that it offered via its BBVA D&A subsidiary. Over the years, BBVA learned that its asset could help urban planners understand the economic impact of city decision-making, disaster recovery managers prioritize relief efforts, and merchants better target and attract customers. In all of these cases, the organizations expected to leverage their data assets to sell any of the following: raw data, prepared data, reports, analytics, or analytics-based consulting services.

Selling might seem to be a good fit for organizations with deep domain expertise and an engaged customer base.[4] However, organizations with an incumbent business model tend to impose the practices and values of their existing business on their selling business. This invariably creates high overhead costs, unnecessary regulatory constraints, bureaucratic processes, rigid data use terms, or conservative talent management practices, any of which can hurt the viability and profitability of an information offering. Organizations need to allow their information businesses to pursue a unique business model without interference. Notably, OM and Kroger both established separate business units to build and nurture their respective cost management and marketing insights businesses. Both companies recognized that selling was different than their respective distribution and retail businesses, and the separate units ensured that information solutions received dedicated managerial attention and resources.

All information solutions fall into one of the same three basic types that improvements and wraps did: they offer data (data solutions),

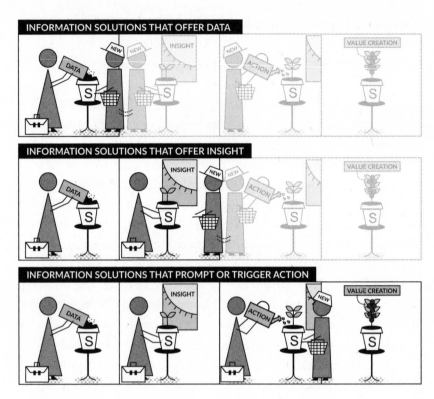

Figure 5.1
How information solutions differ in their scope

insight (insight solutions), or action (action solutions).[5] As with wraps, information solutions create value only in theory until the value-creation process is completed, usually by the customer. As illustrated in figure 5.1, sellers, in addition to having little control over the customer and perhaps knowing too little about the customer, can be far from the action and value creation. That distance can make it hard for selling organizations to price solutions correctly or understand how to evolve and shape the solutions over time.

Information Solutions That Offer Data

Although all kinds of data sets are increasingly available at no cost via "open data" websites and public sector initiatives, selling data is still a huge industry. The global data broker market, which includes companies that collect and sell users' internet information, was valued at US$232 billion in 2019.[6] In 2022, Verisk, Inc., a firm that serves the insurance and energy industries, had 19 petabytes of information in its data stores, an insurance fraud database with more than 1.5 billion claims, and models covering natural hazards in more than one hundred countries.[7] More broadly, the industry includes organizations that specialize in developing unique proprietary data assets by combining multiple data sources, ingesting data from rare sources, generating data based on a platform business or across an ecosystem, or collecting contributory data from a set of peer organizations (often competitors!).[8]

Organizations that focus on data solutions work to create data assets that customers can easily plug into their own data environments. Data assets that customers purchase usually fill gaps in their own data assets, allowing the customer to do analyses or take action that they otherwise could not do. The cheaper and easier it is for customers to access and use the data assets, the more appealing the assets will be to the customers, and thus the more customers will pay for them. For this reason, raw data (data that is minimally processed) rarely will command as high a price as data that has been cleansed, standardized, validated, enhanced, and teed up for analysis.

TRIPBAM, a privately held company in Texas, was founded in 2012 to help travelers reduce their hotel expenses.[9] Over time, it evolved to focus on the corporate travel market, helping organizations' travel units manage travel costs and contract compliance. In 2020, TRIPBAM served the travel needs of roughly half of all Fortune 100 companies. The company offered all three types of information solutions: data, insight, and action. Let's look first at its data offerings.

TRIPBAM developed a portfolio of reports (*data solutions*) that featured information of importance to travel buyers, such as negotiated room rates, amenities adjustments, and corporate program adherence. Large customers paid TRIPBAM a monthly subscription fee to access the reports and other services. During the Covid crisis, TRIPBAM leveraged its visibility into hotel rates to develop novel reports specific to the pandemic. For example, the company launched a weekly closure report that helped its customers know whether a hotel was operating or had shut down (another data solution). TRIPBAM published the closure report for free (such information was of great interest to the industry and policymakers) to demonstrate the value that could be extracted from its data assets.

Information Solutions That Offer Insight

As a consumer, you likely are familiar with the consumer credit score, an insight solution that reveals the likelihood that a person will default on a debt. Companies that provide credit scoring have developed back-end calculations that are proprietary and quite sophisticated. The scores appeal to consumers as well as organizations that offer loans or leases, credit cards, and home mortgages. Employers use them too.

Information solutions that offer insight use analytics to help customers make better decisions. Scores, benchmarks, alerts, and visualizations help customers view and understand data in ways that are tailored to their specific context, helping them prevent or solve problems. However, customers must use the insights—take some action—to find value in them. Therefore, organizations maximize the value potential of their insight offerings by delivering relevant and understandable insights, which fit naturally into their customers' workflows.

When TRIPBAM first entered the hotel rate shopping industry in 2012, it pioneered "clustered rate monitoring" in the hotel industry, which involved monitoring three metrics for a cluster of hotels within a given area: rate fluctuations, the best available rate, and the last-room-available rate. These metrics were the basis for several of its insight solutions. One such solution was to find better hotel rates and suggest rebooking opportunities. Rebooking opportunities were insights that could lower travelers' hotel costs if they rebooked their hotel rooms. Later, when TRIPBAM began serving corporate travel buyers, the company sold insights that informed corporate travel buyers about instances of noncompliance with their hotel rate agreements. But travel buyers still had to follow up with the hotels and attempt to extract refunds. In both cases, the value-creation potential of the insight was quite clear, but customers did not always follow through—take action—and realize savings.

Information Solutions That Prompt or Trigger Action

Ideally, a seller offers information solutions that trigger action by executing a task or by doing something on the customer's behalf. Task automation, process automation, and process outsourcing are ways for sellers to take action on a customer's behalf. These kinds of solutions involve the organization most deeply in customer value creation. In some cases, information solutions simply prompt customers to act on insights by making it very easy or very valuable to do so. Consulting and on-site support are also action-prompting offerings that leverage the organization's accumulated expertise to prompt customer action. The appeal of consulting and on-site support is that both give an organization a front seat view of customer value creation.

Over time, TRIPBAM learned to automate action taking in its solutions when it was possible. For individual travelers, TRIPBAM automatically rebooked hotel stays when a better deal was identified that matched the traveler's preferences and constraints. For travel buyers, when incidences of contract noncompliance were identified, the company generated automatic emails to hotels warning them that they would be removed from the buyer's travel program unless they complied with specific contractual obligations. Facilitating customer action ensured that TRIPBAM's information solutions created value for its customers, and it also made the company's solutions "sticky" because they became embedded in customer habits and processes. Competitors were less appealing to travel buyers who came to consider TRIPBAM reports and services as part of their own standard operating procedures.

For organizations that have advanced data monetization capabilities, automation is achievable. Automation eliminates customer effort in taking action, guaranteeing that the customer will obtain value from the solution. Before customers will accept automated action taking, however, they must have deep trust in the provider's intention and ability. Therefore sellers need to communicate clear rules of engagement that govern automated actions, and they must establish transparent action taking that they can explain and monitor.

When TRIPBAM automated the process of securing the best-value hotel accommodation for travelers for its corporate customers, it was quite a feat. The service had to cancel an existing reservation and move the traveler to a new comparable room at a lower rate while complying with corporate agreements, satisfying traveler preferences, and abiding by hotel cancellation policies. The service resulted from years spent gaining experience with and knowledge about the overall rebooking process, building credibility with its travelers and travel buyers, and investing in technologies that could support fast, secure, and reliable rebooking transactions.

Selling Information Solutions at Healthcare IQ

TRIPBAM's range of data, insight, and action offerings—and its shift to offering action solutions over time—is typical of selling organizations. Let's look at one more seller that experienced a similar journey, this one in the healthcare field.

Healthcare IQ is a privately held healthcare spend management company based in Florida.[10] It was founded to help hospitals manage their data about patient billing. Initially, this meant helping hospitals collect, clean, and standardize their data about patient medical procedures and the associated medical supplies used for those procedures. This was difficult because patient billing data was managed in many different systems, often in inconsistent formats. A hospital could have a single syringe in their systems that looked like twenty distinct products because it was recorded in twenty different ways; Healthcare IQ knew all those ways and could map them to one correct item. Over time, it grew its ability to fix data anomalies like this (using its proprietary product master catalog). The company also amassed a trove of hospital expenditure data and a deep understanding of hospital spend management problems.

Around 2000, the US federal government began to pressure hospitals to manage their costs. By that time, Healthcare IQ's leadership was confident that the company had built up the data monetization capabilities required to compete in the emerging healthcare spend management industry. In addition, leaders believed that the data assets the company had meticulously gathered and curated over the preceding decade (specifically its hospital expenditure data and its product data catalog) could be used to create information solutions that would help hospitals drive down costs.

Healthcare IQ's portfolio of offerings changed over time, beginning with a focus on data solutions and moving to solutions that prompt action.

- *Data solutions:* In its first decade of operation, Healthcare IQ helped hospitals clean and standardize their patient billing data. Over time, it built a team of clinicians who developed tools and processes to enrich its product catalog. The company created new fields that were helpful to hospitals, such as a product equivalency field that indicated which products could be interchanged without concern.

- *Insight solutions:* Healthcare IQ's offerings evolved to include a web-based reporting interface that helped hospitals benchmark their spending against the spending of other hospitals and medical entities. Over time, Healthcare IQ incorporated interface visualizations, alerting, and exception reporting to better highlight for customers precisely what they should be learning from the reports. In 2011, Healthcare IQ rolled out Colours IQ, a Google Maps–like experience based on a proprietary tool that delivered data visualizations via hundreds of thousands of predefined pivot tables. Colours IQ helped users identify and evaluate potential savings opportunities using visual features, such as colors, to indicate spend levels that were above or below expectations.

- *Action-prompting solutions:* By 2014, Healthcare IQ offered on-site consulting services to help customers take appropriate actions based on the insights in its reporting tools. Consultants were placed with hospital teams to help the teams access, interpret, and act on savings opportunities. To convince hospital leaders to buy its consulting service, Healthcare IQ offered a shared-savings model, earning revenues based on how much it could help the hospital save.

Creating Value from Selling

Like wrapping, selling creates value at the hands of the customer after the customer acts on the seller's data, insight, or action solutions. But this does not mean that selling organizations passively wait around for that to happen—quite the opposite. Experienced sellers know how the customer value-creation process should unfold, including how the information solution will get used. These sellers also come to expect that a customer will sometimes drop the ball. Sellers constantly analyze customer behaviors, sentiments, and needs, proactively monitoring data or insight access, tool usage, or action taking. When monitoring is proactive, the seller will have time to fix any failure to act using education, product design, customer service, or incentives. As with wrapping organizations, selling organizations often choose to offer solutions further down the data-insight-action value process.

Because selling often involves seizing new market opportunities, new customers are usually in the mix. It follows that this new customer's value-creation process and desired customer experience will take some time for the seller to appreciate. Here, too, collaborative development can ensure value creation. As with wraps, information solutions benefit from development approaches that leverage collaborative customer relationships. They allow the seller to learn what value the customer is creating and how.

In the case of TRIPBAM, company leaders focused on delivering a compelling ROI to their customers. To monitor this, they computed a client-specific ROI by tracking each customer's savings compared to how much the client paid TRIPBAM for services. Not surprisingly, TRIPBAM had virtually no customer churn.

Realizing Value from Selling

Information solutions, like wraps, are typically priced starting with a careful analysis of how much value is created for the customer. The solution cannot be priced beyond its potential value to the customer, at least not for long. For example, Healthcare IQ expected a US$100 million hospital to achieve at least US$2–3 million in cost savings; TRIPBAM tried to deliver 2–3 percent in overall savings on its customers' total travel spend (which could be as much as US$10 million). With knowledge of potential customer value in hand, organizations can choose a pricing strategy that makes sense for their specific information solutions and will work for the customers buying them.

Data solutions are often viewed and priced as commodities. If there are only a few customers for a data solution, one way to price the data is at auction. For example, an investment bank that wants to predict market trends more accurately might be willing to pay top dollar on auction for exclusive rights to a rare data asset. Those buying data at auction probably know precisely what it is worth to them. In the case of investment banks, it could be millions of dollars.

Pricing information solutions that offer insight or that trigger action is challenging. Still, cocreating with a few customers, monitoring use, or providing consulting services to them can afford an insider view of the customer experience. Initially, selling organizations might establish a shared value agreement whereby they take on the costs and risk of developing an information solution for a customer in return for some percentage of value that materializes for the customer. In these cases, sellers often develop offerings that prompt or trigger action to ensure value creation, the tree of fruit to be shared. TRIPBAM offered value-sharing deals to its smaller clients that could not reliably predict the number of monitored reservations they would need and didn't want to overpay for TRIPBAM's monthly subscription services. The gainsharing model entitled TRIPBAM to receive 25 percent of the realized savings for any reservation that it rebooked on the smaller client's behalf.

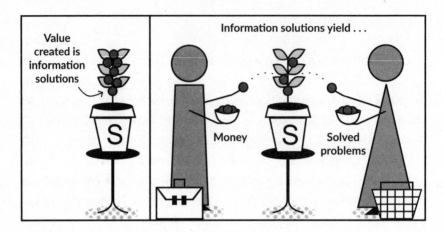

Figure 5.2
Value realization from selling initiatives

As with wrapping, information solutions create value, some of which is realized for the organization in the form of money and some of which goes home with the customer whose problems are solved, as shown in figure 5.2. And, as always, some value is left on the tree, so to speak; some value is created but not turned into money by the organization. In the case of information solutions, that value might take the form of brand capital, good customer relationships, or innovative capacity. And, as noted earlier, the amount of value that can be realized cannot exceed the amount of value created. You can only pick as much fruit as is on the tree.

Another consideration when pricing information solutions is the position of the information solution in a competitive marketplace. What a customer is willing to pay depends on both how much potential value the solution promises (assuming the value-creation process will happen) and the price of alternative solutions. (If the solution is competitively distinct, alternatives don't matter, but how much value the customer expects to create does.) An information solution—like any type of offering—is competitively distinct when it is rare, cannot be imitated, and can withstand the threat of substitutes.[11] For example, when Healthcare IQ's offerings were first on the market, they were one of a kind, so they were definitely rare.

A competitively distinct solution is difficult to imitate. Often, its mechanics are complex, hidden, or protected from imitation by patents. Healthcare IQ worked with a technology partner to develop a unique visualization offering that their hospital customers loved. It was easy to understand and use, but it was not easy to reverse engineer or recreate from scratch. Healthcare IQ's CEO believed so strongly in the underlying technology, called fractal maps, that he purchased the fractal map company so that Healthcare IQ would hold the fifty-plus patents associated with the technology. The CEO wanted to prevent competitors from partnering with that same tech company to create similar solutions.

A competitively distinct solution can withstand the threat of substitutes. It's hard for customers to find a comparable replacement. An organization can do this by developing features and benefits that customers can't find elsewhere. This is a key reason why sellers also do a lot of wrapping! They rely on wrapping to boost a solution's customer value proposition again and again.

In fact, the biggest threat to information solutions is the copycat provider—the cheaper substitute. Because of this risk, an organization not only needs to offer a unique and desirable information solution but also must maintain the solution's uniqueness and desirability over time. Otherwise, revenue streams will dry up. Years ago, when Magid Abraham, then CEO of Comscore, was speaking to a class about selling information solutions, he said, quite passionately, "Information products are obsolete upon launch!"[12] The information solution marketplace can be ruthlessly competitive. Competitive pressures force information businesses to continuously innovate and improve their information solutions so they can keep their solutions distinct from those of competitors.

So, how do information businesses create solutions that maintain their competitive advantage over time? They draw on the following sources of value that allow them to create offerings that are rare, difficult to replicate, and difficult to substitute:[13]

- Unique data that is sourced, combined, or enhanced to produce one-of-a-kind data assets.

- Cost-effective, proprietary platforms that can process data and do things that competitors simply can't do or can't do as cheaply. Proprietary platforms are notoriously difficult to reverse engineer.
- Sophisticated data science and data scientists who are passionate about solving problems with data. While one algorithm might be replicable or substitutable, a complex combination of algorithms that is the brainchild of sophisticated data scientists is far less likely to be.
- Domain expertise that sellers promote by having their domain experts speak at conferences, sit on standards boards, and publish industry white papers and academic articles.
- Customer empathy that helps sellers understand and appreciate customer problems deeply. It also helps them identify ways to monitor and measure their ability to create customer value.

Note that these sources of value are rooted in data monetization capabilities. This is yet another reason organizations engaged in selling initiatives need advanced capabilities.

Capability Considerations for Selling

While Healthcare IQ developed a successful business model around selling, selling is still inherently higher risk than improving or wrapping. Selling organizations face the need to develop and grow new markets, the need to establish a new business model, the need to keep up with data privacy laws, and the need to constantly fend off competitive threats. To overcome these challenges, organizations that sell information solutions rely heavily on advanced enterprise data monetization capabilities in all five areas, as can be seen in figure 5.3.[14]

Organizations that are top performers in selling information solutions report having the following data monetization capabilities:

- Unique, high-quality data assets that are easily combinable, including with their customers' data.
- Advanced technology data platforms that offer secure, fast, and reliable access to both internal and external users.

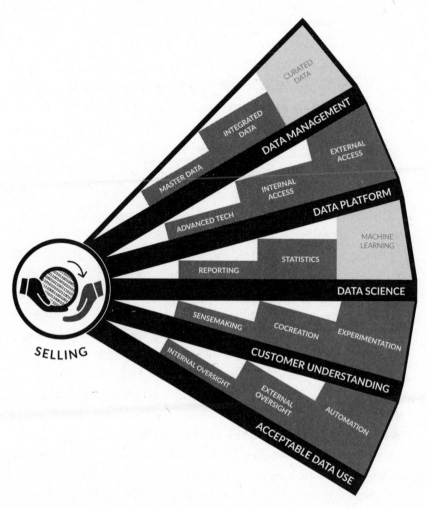

Figure 5.3
The capabilities of top-performing selling organizations

- The ability to use statistics to extract sophisticated insights from vast quantities of data.

- The ability to experiment with solutions to uncover customer needs and wants so that new market needs are constantly served with appealing offerings with a high likelihood of creating customer value.

- Automated data use controls that ensure the protection and oversight of sensitive and valuable information at scale.

The final point warrants further attention. Modern life has become highly quantifiable and connected. As a result, data assets that are used to develop information solutions can contain sensitive data. They can reflect the behaviors of individuals as customers, citizens, employees, students, and activists. As of this writing, too many organizations lack adequate local, federal, and global safeguards associated with data asset sourcing, manipulation, use, and protection. Having an advanced acceptable data use capability is critical to navigating ethical challenges.[15] An organization must have an enterprise ability to make sure that data asset use is not only compliant with regulations but also consistent with the values of its stakeholders. In fact, when considering ethics, companies might want to be more restrictive with their data than current regulations stipulate. Regrettably, a deeper treatment of this complex topic is outside the scope of this book.

As noted earlier, more advanced capabilities are associated with better data monetization outcomes. In the case of selling initiatives, however, advanced capabilities are a requirement rather than an option.

Data Monetization Capabilities at Healthcare IQ

When people look under the hood of an information business, they often are surprised by the sophistication and innovation of the data monetization practices they see. Such practices are often a necessity. A selling organization might have a hard time finding commercial technology powerful enough to process its massive amount of data, so it builds its own hardware and software. A selling organization might need to establish credibility before entering a new market with a solution, so it hires the most highly regarded data scientist in the field. A selling organization might need to reassure its investors of the security of its sensitive data assets, so it establishes data oversight methodologies that go well beyond regulatory requirements. Regardless of whether a seller needed to adopt innovative and sophisticated practices or simply thought it wise to do so, it's fair to say that advanced data monetization capabilities are part of the game at well-established selling organizations.

This was certainly the case at Healthcare IQ. Over time, by need and by choice, the company adopted increasingly advanced ways to manage, distribute, and oversee its data assets and effectively serve customers. Leaders relied on technologists, systems integrators, content specialists, sales account managers, and customer service providers to propose helpful practices—or identify needs for practices—and incorporate them into operations.

Healthcare IQ established a *data management capability* as it developed a way to standardize, match, and validate data ingested from its hospital customers' transaction systems. At first, data problems were fixed manually. Then as the team gradually identified the root causes of problems, it established business rules and automated the fixing using custom workflow software, resulting in increasingly cleaner data assets over time. The company also developed tools and processes to enrich the data. Enrichment activities ranged from mapping products to the correct manufacturer, reviewing and tagging products for equivalency, and classifying products so that analysts at Healthcare IQ's hospital customers could develop better reports.

At the heart of Healthcare IQ's *data platform capability* was a proprietary custom-built data warehouse that was managed by technologists with skills in data architecture, virtualization, database development, infrastructure, open source, and software engineering. The technologists learned how to serve the company's internal data processing and distribution needs as well as the needs of hospital customers. For the latter, they built out faster and more efficient ways for the hospitals' IT people to submit hospital data; for example, they developed a simple interface that hospitals could use to check whether their data files met Healthcare IQ loading specifications. This avoided subsequent problems that might have occurred from bad, mislabeled, or missing data fields.

Healthcare IQ was ingesting data from multiple hospital customers, so it began to develop data assets based on this aggregated data (after securing permission to do so). Data analysts used the assets to calculate benchmarks and indices and to create reports to solve a hospital's cost management problems. As mentioned earlier, in 2011, Healthcare IQ introduced Colours IQ, an advanced analytics tool that delivered data visualizations via hundreds of thousands of predefined pivot tables. The CEO viewed the tool as an essential contribution to the company's *data science capability*. Several years later, Healthcare IQ hired an AI expert to explore ways for the company to benefit from machine learning.

Healthcare IQ sales and service teams were instrumental in building the company's *customer understanding capability*. The team members interacted with customers during weekly phone calls, informal conversations, and emails; cocreated novel offerings with customers during consulting engagements; and learned about customer needs during quarterly business reviews, on-site training, and routine support. For example, during support, a customer might ask for a particular attribute to be added to a report. Team members mined support experiences to identify ways to add functionality to existing products, develop new offerings, or automate customer processes, submitting ideas to a system that tracked them. Management discussed and prioritized submitted ideas at a weekly staff meeting, and ultimately, high-priority ideas flowed into product development. To get deeper insight into customers, Healthcare IQ hired people who previously worked in customer or partner organizations when it could.

Finally, Healthcare IQ developed its *acceptable data use capability* to ensure that hospitals were comfortable with the company's guardianship of their data. Initially, Healthcare IQ established HIPAA-compliant processes, policies, and procedures. Later, leaders pursued HITRUST certification, which would corroborate Healthcare IQ's conformance with security best practices. The company sought external validation of its efforts, and it promoted such confirmation to customers, partners, and other stakeholders.

Healthcare IQ's advanced data monetization capabilities positioned the company to cope with the turbulent dynamics of the health-care spend market. Hospitals that had historically focused on under-standing their costs were prompted by new US government regulation to understand their costs within the context of clinical outcomes. New competitors—including software providers, consultants, distributors, industry associations, and start-ups—began to offer spend analysis solu-tions to their hospital customers. Customer expectations grew as hos-pitals developed savvier talent and modernized their systems. Despite such strong forces, Healthcare IQ drew on its capabilities to adapt accordingly and stay competitive.

Ownership of Selling Initiatives

Like wrapping initiatives, selling initiatives should also be led by a prod-uct owner. However, in the case of selling, the "product" is an informa-tion solution. (Remember, this book uses the term *information solution owner* to distinguish between wrapping and selling owners.) Informa-tion solution owners manage an informational product with its own value proposition, whereas product owners use wraps to enhance their core product's value proposition.

An information solution owner is accountable for the overall profit-ability of the revenue streams associated with selling. Because of the specialized expertise needed for this type of role, organizations often recruit seasoned professionals from information businesses, technology companies, or successful digital-native companies to be information solution owners. These people bring a solid customer-centric mindset and experience in planning, developing, and delivering information offerings to the role. The information solution owner manages the costs, risks, and benefits associated with the information solution.

You can think of an information solution owner as the mini-CEO of an information solution, coordinating the disparate activities required to produce, market, and sustain it, including solution design, compliance, sales, marketing, and IT services. Like a CEO, the owner of an information solution depends on expertise and commitment from across the enterprise. In an information business or a business unit devoted to information solutions, virtually every employee is involved in some aspect of the information solutions: design, compliance, sales, marketing, after-sales service, and, last but not least, IT services. So it should not surprise you that selling organizations employ people at all levels who deeply understand the customer problem domain—whether it be hospital health costs or hotel travel spend—and passionately want to help customers solve problems using data. As a result, selling, too, is everybody's business!

Time to Reflect

In theory, every organization that has data can use it to create data assets that can give rise to information solutions. If your organization wants to pursue the selling approach, start with important problems that someone, somewhere, will pay your organization to solve. Here are the key points from this chapter to keep in mind:

- Instead of thinking about ways to sell your vast troves of data, think about what customer problems could be solved using your data assets. *Who in your organization knows the most about the important problems customers are struggling to solve?*

- Once you've identified a customer problem that your organization could solve as long as the customer took some specific action, you will need to work to ensure that the customer actually takes that action and realizes value from it. *Which of your customers might work closely with someone in your organization on this?*

- It's essential that your organization's information solutions be competitively distinctive. *What distinctive assets does your organization have that would make your information solution rare, hard to imitate, or difficult to do without?*

- Organizations that are adept at selling have high levels of data monetization capabilities. *Where is your organization in terms of accumulating these capabilities? Which capabilities need to be addressed first? What would be the best way to go about building these capabilities?*
- To offer an information solution, you must establish a supporting business model. *Where in your organization would you find the new market development, product strategy, and other kinds of expertise your information business would need?*

You should now have a good handle on the range of data monetization initiatives that can make money for your organization— improving, wrapping, and selling—and what it takes to pull them off. In the next chapter, you will learn about the ideal organization context for data monetization: a data democracy.

6 Creating a Data Democracy

The more we increase access to data, the more we enable curiosity and innovation.

—Rob Samuel, CVS Health

At BBVA, Microsoft, PepsiCo, Healthcare IQ, and all the organizations you have read about so far, people of all kinds are inspired to engage in data monetization. They are rewarded for questioning the status quo, sharing ideas, adopting novel practices, changing habits, and contributing to organizational goals. They believe that data is valuable, is essential, and plays a role in the organization's success. This kind of organization, so conducive to making money from data, is called a *data democracy*.

It takes a lot of effort to get the average employee ready and willing to participate in the data monetization movement. Part of the challenge is rooted in the old problem of data versus domain knowledge. Domain experts (accountants, marketers, nurses, civil servants, factory workers, sales associates—anyone with expertise in a part of an organization) and data experts (analysts, data scientists, dashboard designers, database administrators) each have something important to offer to an improving, wrapping, or selling initiative. For example, to fix a process glitch, you need a process manager to interpret the problem and a software developer to write the code. But before coding can start, the developer must understand the problem and the process manager must recognize the potential of data assets and data monetization capabilities. It's tricky to come to a common problem understanding, using the same language, and to agree on the optimal use of these *data monetization resources*. Turf battles, skill gaps, and politics get in the way. Nevertheless, leaders of data democracies actively manage through these hurdles and design their organizations for success.

> Data monetization resources *are the full set of resources that speed up data monetization initiatives, including data assets and data monetization capabilities. Data monetization capabilities may be found in people with expertise or expertise embedded in tools, routines, policies, forms, software, and so on.*

In short, your organization won't become a data democracy organically. Data and domain experts must be motivated to learn from each other. Without a deep understanding of the organization's needs, data experts will be hard pressed to develop the most useful data monetization capabilities and the most reusable data assets. Shared knowledge— more data savvy among domain experts and more domain savvy among data experts—is the key to valuable innovation as well as the diffusion of those innovations—scaling and reusing them. Innovation and the diffusion of innovation are achievable in data democracies. This chapter describes the specific organizational design elements that underpin a successful and sustainable data democracy: data-domain connections and data democracy incentives.[1]

> *A* data democracy *is an organization with pervasive employee appreciation of, access to, and use of an organization's reusable data assets and data monetization capabilities (i.e., its data monetization resources).*[2]

A question to ask yourself

What keeps your domain and data experts from collaborating to leverage your organization's data monetization resources?

Data-Domain Connections

Imagine that all the "data" people in an organization were colored red and all the "domain" people were colored blue. As these red and blue people regularly interact, share what they know, and learn from each other, their knowledge blends and they become less red or blue and more purple. They develop a shared grasp of data in their particular organizational context. A data democracy is populated by purple people![3]

Organizational design is commonly thought of as the way in which workflows, authority relationships, and social ties are organized within the organization. In the case of data democracy, workflows, authority relationships, and social ties are configured into structures that blend red and blue people. The blending occurs by virtue of *data-domain connections*: organizational structures linking data experts and domain experts that facilitate knowledge exchange and learning.

Data-domain connections *are structures that facilitate knowledge exchange between data experts and domain experts.*

Dr. Ida A. Someh, a long-time collaborator of the book's author team, studied how relationships between analytics groups and business-domain groups can be configured to facilitate knowledge integration in data-driven organizational initiatives. She found five common data-domain connections: embedded experts, multidisciplinary teams, shared services, social networks, and advisory services. (See figure 6.1.) These five connections are different means of knowledge sharing—

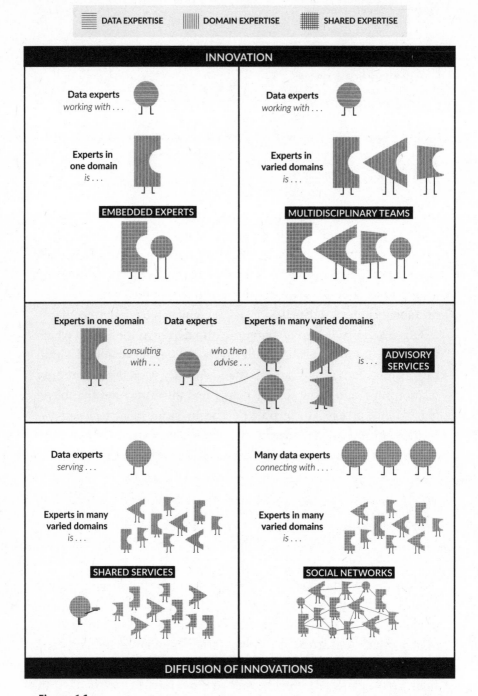

Figure 6.1
Five data-domain connections that facilitate knowledge exchange and learning

creating purple people—crucial to both innovation and the diffusion of innovations across the organization. They work differently, and they work together. Think of these connections as tools in your organizational design toolkit, the data democracy special edition toolkit. Organizations can use any and all of the five connecting structures; ideally, organizations should support enough structures to yield as much of a data democracy as they need.

The connections facilitate two-way collaboration, conversations, and learning. They build on and help consolidate any knowledge gained in formal training experiences. For example, if a domain expert takes a statistics course, a data expert can help to apply that new skill to a particular problem. If a data expert takes a course in marketing, a domain expert from marketing can help contextualize concepts from the course to the specific organization. The connections make it easier for domain experts to become aware of, access, and use data assets and data monetization capabilities as they engage in improving, wrapping, and selling initiatives. The connections also make it easier for data experts to understand how to make data monetization resources more valuable to the organization. The more knowledge transfer is activated, the more organizations can fully develop and exploit superior data monetization resources. When data democracy is advancing too slowly and data monetization assets and capabilities are stuck in silos, organizational leaders might find it beneficial to introduce a few additional connecting structures. Let's step through each one in turn.

Innovation Connections

Two of the connections link data and domain people in ways that foster innovation: embedded experts and multidisciplinary teams. (See the top of figure 6.1.) With innovation connections, data and domain people exchange knowledge and generate new and improved tasks and processes and new and enhanced products and solutions.

For example, when an organization embeds a data expert full time in a marketing department, it is easier for marketing employees to find new ways to exploit existing data assets in their daily work. Thus, the organizational capacity to envision and undertake big new initiatives gets stronger. Maybe the data expert knows how to use an algorithm to identify a "next-best offer" (the most relevant thing to offer a particular customer at that moment). The data expert would help the marketers experiment with using this algorithm to target offerings to different customer segments. The result will be new knowledge on both sides of the connection: the data person will know more about this marketing situation, and the marketing people will know more about next-best offer algorithms. They will both be a little more purple. With a better understanding on both sides, the marketing department (including the embedded data expert) might begin testing the effectiveness of AI-suggested next-best offers. The test results might inspire a new improving initiative to make the process of selecting next-best offers faster and more precise, potentially reducing some costs and increasing sales. This is how embedded experts foster innovation.

Similarly, when an organization assembles a multidisciplinary team to carry out some initiative, perhaps one to solve a customer churn problem, they are ensuring that both data and domain perspectives (a variety of domain perspectives, probably) will inform the solution. Picture this: marketers in an organization are stuck in a rut and are using outdated tools for managing customer churn. A multidisciplinary team is formed, charged with proposing a machine learning approach for customer churn management. The data scientists would share contemporary ways to predict customer churn based on both internal and external data. Sales domain people would explain how salespeople currently connect with customers to keep them satisfied. Marketers would contribute timeless customer retention principles. As the team members share and absorb new knowledge, they formulate ideas about managing customer churn and propose an improving initiative. Notably, not only does the multidisciplinary team develop a meaningful data monetization initiative that solves the customer churn problem, but the people on the team have each become more purple. These purple people are more capable of accessing, contextualizing, and using data related to customer churn and machine learning to create new innovations.

Diffusion of Innovation Connections

If an organization only draws on embedded data experts and multi-disciplinary teams, then over time, localized silos of innovation will proliferate. This is why connections that promote the diffusion of innovations—shared services and social networks—are essential. (See the bottom of figure 6.1.) These connections help spread innovations of all shapes and sizes to other parts of the organization. Diffusion occurs when people reuse, rather than reinvent, innovations that exploit data assets and capabilities. The reuse of process improvements across similar organizational contexts is one way to increase the value created and realized from an improving initiative. Wraps can also be reused across related product lines if additional product managers become aware of them. Sometimes diffusion happens spontaneously because an innovation (e.g., a new platform that eliminates paper-based processing) is such an obvious improvement that it's an easy move to replace the status quo. But usually, even a brilliant new or improved tool, process, or product needs a nudge to spread because spreading is rarely completely costless (e.g., people need training to use the new platform).

When an organization sets up a shared service unit to deliver standard reporting software and templates, it is making it easier for domain people to apply those tools, adopting them as is or customizing them. Shared services are great for diffusing innovations far and wide; they offer a one-to-many relationship. For example, say the organization's product-line unit creates a dazzling sales dashboard that people in other units drool over. A shared services group (the one) can spread the dazzle to any other unit that is eager for their own drool-worthy dashboards (the many). In addition, the shared services group can offer features like common dashboard metrics with suggested data sources; ideal colors, visuals, and other user interface tactics; and self-service options for dashboarding training.

Social networks, on the other hand, use many-to-many relationships to diffuse innovations. These connections bring together red and blue employees with common interests but different knowledge. Using social networks, data and domain people can ask each other questions and provide answers. Social networks can be virtual, like a Slack community, or physical, like a data science conference or event.

The Advisory Services Connection

There is one data-domain connection—advisory services—that facilitates both innovation and diffusion. (See the middle of figure 6.1.) It's a super connection and works like a consulting model: consultants learn from their current engagement so they can spread lessons and practices to future engagements. Everybody learns, especially the consultant. More people turn purple, and the data democracy grows.

A lot of organizations have advisory services. They are often centers of excellence that work with people all over the organization to solve specific problems. Sometimes advisory services are part of the enterprise hub of a data transformation office or in the chief data office. Centers of excellence can also be smaller and more local, serving a specific organization area, like research and development or a vertical line of business. Wherever they sit, the advisory services people transfer knowledge to and from their own unit, learning about organizational needs and spreading new knowledge about data monetization resources throughout the organization. They spread the wealth, so to speak.

Note that some organizations create this one structure (often as an enterprise center of excellence) and stop there. This results in innovation and diffusion of innovations for sure—but not enough of it. In large organizations, a single advisory services connection will quickly become a bottleneck and slow down the growth of a data democracy.

Connecting Structures at Microsoft

Chapter 3 described several improving initiatives that were underway at Microsoft when the company first shifted its business model from being product based to delivering cloud services.[4] Remember how finance shortened the time it took to get financial analyses into the hands of sales personnel? And how enterprise sales reduced the administrative workload of salespeople to give them more time for customer-facing activities?

The total number of improving initiatives and the amount of innovation introduced at Microsoft during this time was staggering. One of the reasons for the abundance of activity was the company's thoughtful use of organization design.[5] Microsoft used all five connecting structures to facilitate improving initiatives and elevate people's ability to exploit their enterprise data assets and data monetization capabilities, which fueled the company's business model transformation. In addition, these same connecting structures ensured that the data monetization resources that were made available to initiative teams were what those teams needed.

Microsoft used embedded experts and multidisciplinary teams to help develop new work processes and new data capabilities. For example, the data experts embedded within the enterprise sales unit were instrumental in establishing the Microsoft Sales Experience platform and helping develop the new enterprise sales processes that the salesforce wanted. Other units like HR and marketing had similar embedded teams of experts and enjoyed similar innovative outcomes.

At times, people from different parts of Microsoft came together in multidisciplinary teams to achieve a target goal. For example, the data science group and facilities organization—with support from people in legal and HR—collaborated to optimize the company's energy consumption. This team needed to be multidisciplinary because the problem it was solving—designing "smart" building heating and cooling solutions—was a multidisciplinary problem.

Nadella himself leveraged a kind of multidisciplinary team to develop a dashboard with metrics that served as leading indicators for the key pillars of the Microsoft business. To help identify new data sources to generate the metrics, he hosted an internal dashboard-building hackathon. Business units across Microsoft collaborated on building a senior management dashboard; the effort identified both the systems that held critical data and the business owners accountable for results. The effort resulted in a new approach to measuring the success of Microsoft's transition to a cloud services business model.

As innovations sprang up in one place, Microsoft leveraged shared services to diffuse innovations that would benefit others. For example, leadership invested in data-specific shared services groups, including one for business intelligence that delivered templates, standard ways of reporting, and dashboarding across the company. Other shared services groups were responsible for diffusing other kinds of innovations: standard sales territory geographies (owned by the data management services group), building occupancy-related AI models (owned by the data science services group), and emergent policies to comply with new General Data Protection Regulation (GDPR) requirements (owned by the data governance services group).

The business intelligence services group created social network communities using Microsoft's own social network platform so that users with shared interests and concerns could engage with one another to surface challenges and share ideas. These communities exchanged novel ways of reporting data and deriving insights; these innovations had previously only been used in the local business units where they originated.

Finally, Microsoft benefited from the innovation and diffusion effects of advisory structures. For example, the CIO established a dashboard team that consulted with Microsoft business executives to help them with their dashboards. The dashboard team sat down with each executive and created dashboards customized to their needs and preferences, resulting in widespread dashboard rollout and use. As a result, these advisors got increasingly in tune with senior management's dashboarding needs, continually learning new ways to meet those needs and delivering better and more helpful support.

Data Democracy Incentives

To achieve their data democracy goals, leaders must do more than put a smart organizational design in place. They also need to ensure that people interact with their data or domain counterparts and learn from each other—especially about the availability of reusable data assets and data monetization capabilities. Employees may have little time or inclination to interact with others, never mind engage in improving, wrapping, and selling initiatives. Leaders must activate a smart organization design by providing incentives to people so they will engage in connecting, innovating, and diffusing those innovations. Otherwise, any emerging new processes or offerings (if there are any) will not become the new normal across the board.

To encourage people to seek out new knowledge and learn from their available connections, organizations should consider using incentives to induce employees to move the organization toward a data democracy. As illustrated in figure 6.2, power, social norms, and value propositions are three types of incentives that organizations can use to motivate employees to become more purple so they can make full use of data monetization resources.

Power

Leaders can use the power inherent in their formal or informal authority to get their employees to adopt and use analytics tools, attend training, or contribute their experiences to forums. (See the top of figure 6.2.) Leaders use formal power when they require behavioral change and informal power when they make it clear that they expect all employees to change their behavior. They communicate these expectations by linking performance evaluations to data use and by recognizing and rewarding employees' success with data.

Nadella, for example, clearly signaled his expectations by being an enthusiastic early adopter of the dashboard created in Microsoft's dashboard-building hackathon. He began actively using the dashboard to inform his decisions, and leaders across the company soon followed suit. Once Microsoft's business intelligence platform was widely available, business unit leaders became accountable for their employees' dashboard use. If adoption wasn't 100 percent, leaders contacted the employees' managers, soliciting a plan to remediate. Microsoft's

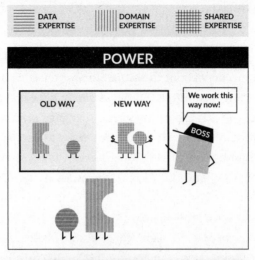

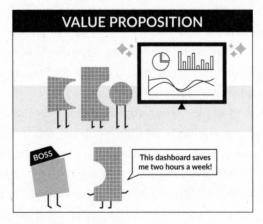

Figure 6.2
Three kinds of data democracy incentives

management also established new performance metrics to push the use of connecting structures: they adjusted employee incentives to include "collaboration across workgroups" as one of the three core pillars on which individuals were assessed and rewarded.

Social Norms

Employees are more likely to use a new dashboard, call on a customer based on an analytics-based alert, or search the enterprise data catalog for a new data source when their peers are doing the same thing, especially if their peers can assuage their misgivings. (See the middle of figure 6.2.) There is a virtuous circle effect to social norm motivation: employees provide help and support to their peers and, in so doing, raise expectations that others will follow suit. For example, Microsoft's internal social network, Yammer, served as a source of peer support for using the company's dashboarding tool. Yammer exchanges about the tool encouraged employees to embrace the tool while also providing support for those who were having trouble adapting it for their specific needs.

Microsoft leveraged social norms, in part, by making the adoption of data-fueled decisions visible. Nadella's hackathon-built dashboard included a scorecard based on data supplied by many, but not all, business units across the company. After the scorecard was launched, business units that hadn't initially contributed data rushed to do so; they, too, wanted a presence on the CEO's dashboard.

Value Proposition

Leaders tasked with driving new data monetization initiatives often find themselves trying to win over colleagues to get them to contribute people or funding to it. A clear value proposition—what data monetization outcomes will mean to those involved in the initiative—can encourage people to participate in a new improving, wrapping, or selling initiative. (See the bottom of figure 6.2.) The value proposition becomes clear when leaders share success stories that showcase valuable outcomes for many stakeholders. A clear value proposition is particularly apropos for initiatives where multidisciplinary teams are needed—each of those distinct disciplines (or domains) might be seeking different outcomes!

Microsoft took active steps to articulate the value proposition inherent to its transformation. Nadella frequently spoke about the role and value of data in the company's transformation, both to external stakeholders and within the company. Across the company, business leaders articulated the value proposition that was specific to their people. In the case of enterprise sales, for example, sales leaders spoke about how the Microsoft Sales Experience platform made work simpler and more fruitful for employees who were engaged in fieldwork. As employees used the system and became better at recording data about their customer interactions, they noticed that predictions and alerts regarding their customers grew more accurate and helpful. And, as a result, they closed more sales. The value propositions associated with the transformation were clearly communicated, and they triggered changes in behavior.

People need to be persuaded and encouraged to support their organization's desire to innovate with data. Incentives like power, social norms, and value propositions can increase the likelihood that people will connect with their data or domain colleagues and share expertise and data monetization resources.

Time to Reflect

Organizations become data democracies by removing barriers for domain experts to become aware of, access, and use data assets and capabilities and for data experts to learn how to develop the right ones. This transformation results in a broad upsurge in the organization's ability to exploit data assets. Leaders who link data and domain people enable knowledge sharing, inspire learning, and generate innovations of all kinds. Connections that link local efforts with centralized efforts help surface and sync up localized innovations so they can be publicized and scaled across the organization. To activate connections, leaders can institute "carrot and stick" techniques such as establishing award programs that recognize employees for using data (a carrot) and establishing accountability for data use when evaluating employee performance (a stick). Here are the key points from this chapter to keep in mind:

- In a data democracy, everybody in the organization can participate in data monetization initiatives. *Where in your organization are people willing and able to be part of an improving, wrapping, or selling initiative?*

- Organizations use five data-domain connections to unleash innovation and the diffusion of knowledge. *Which of the connections are most commonly found in your organization? How can you develop other forms of connection?*

- In a data democracy, everybody in the organization knows how to access and use the organization's data assets and data monetization capabilities, if they need them. *What organizational structures are most helpful in connecting people with capabilities in your organization?*

- Even in a democracy, people need the motivation to embrace learning from others and to change their habits. *Which incentives is your organization using to encourage more fruitful use of data assets? What additional incentives should your organization consider adopting?*

- Innovations that are diffused as widely as possible deliver much greater payback. *Reflect on a recent experience working on any data initiative where the team developed new practices, such as a process to automate data quality. Did that practice spread to other initiative teams or not? If yes, what connections or incentives were in place? If not, what barriers were in place?*

This chapter focused on describing the two key elements of a data democracy. There is one more thing to know about data democracies: they need direction. The next chapter is about developing a guiding vision for your data monetization strategy.

7 Data Monetization Strategy

> Having a data monetization strategy is devilishly helpful. It forces
> you to be clear in your thinking. It also helps you decide what to do.
> —David Lamond, Scentre Group

You've read about the five data monetization capabilities (data management, data platform, data science, customer understanding, and
acceptable data use), the three kinds of data monetization initiatives
(improving, wrapping, and selling), and the five data democracy connections that facilitate organizational innovation and diffusion. Put
into action, these frameworks will propel your organization forward,
but first you must ask, Where do we want to go?

The frameworks serve as avenues that can lead an organization
toward different ends. The same framework components can solve different problems or achieve different objectives. You'll need a north star
to chart a clear course. Remember the CarMax example from chapter
1? Every CarMax employee contributes to the collective mission: either
they are trying to sell more cars or they are trying to buy more cars.
What's important to your organization? Without a north star, it's hard
to discern the answer to questions like the following: Which should we
pursue, improving or selling? Which capability needs the most attention, data science or customer understanding? Which parts of our organization need to be better connected to data assets and capabilities?

You can think of the frameworks as ingredients laid out before a
skilled chef (that's you!). The chef can combine the ingredients into

several different delectable dishes. But to get started, she needs a vision for the meal and an understanding of what type of palate it should satisfy. Then she will know where to begin.

Frameworks (ingredients) in hand, you now need a *data monetization strategy*. A strategy includes a goal and a plan for reaching that goal. This chapter focuses on finding a north star—a vision—for what the organization hopes to accomplish by monetizing data. A strategy for data monetization sheds light on the best application of the data monetization frameworks and what outcomes to expect from applying them. The clearer your north star, the more focused you can be as you build capabilities, invest in initiatives, and design your data democracy.

> A data monetization strategy *is a high-level plan that communicates how an organization will improve its bottom line using its data assets. It is a component of an organization's data strategy.*

Questions to ask yourself

Does your organization have a data monetization strategy today? If so, who was responsible for developing it and sharing its contents?

Setting Direction with a Data Monetization Strategy

Strategies are high-level plans that communicate what goals an organization wants to achieve and how it will achieve those goals. A strategy focuses resources, energy, and attention on some objectives rather than others.[1] No organization can "do it all" because no organization has limitless resources and managerial attention. All organizations, instead, are constrained by fixed amounts of money, people, time, energy, enthusiasm, patience, you name it. As a result, organizations rely on clear strategies to help people decide when to say yes or no, where to spend their time, and what results to track.

A *business strategy* outlines an organization's plan for achieving specific business goals. A *digital strategy* is a plan that focuses on goals related to digital technology and digital ways of working. It explains what an organization will invest in to achieve those goals. A *data strategy* lays out an organization's goals and plans for managing and exploiting its data.[2] It's a tall order to juggle and integrate so many diverse plans. It therefore helps to think of all these strategies as nesting into each other (see figure 7.1). In fact, the elements of a *data monetization*

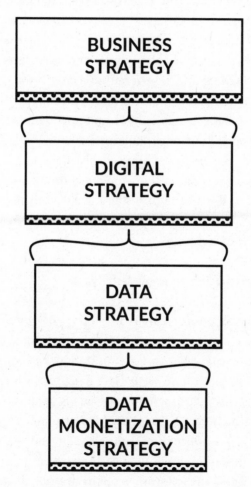

Figure 7.1
A data monetization strategy as a component of an overall business strategy

strategy—data monetization initiatives, data monetization capabilities, and efforts to establish a data democracy—serve as critical pieces of a general data strategy. (There are plenty of other elements that would be found in an organization's data strategy, which would address issues like data security, vendor sourcing, and talent management.)

Different readers will find themselves in different strategic situations. Some will work for organizations with clear business strategies that their leaders regularly articulate and reinforce. Others will struggle to find direction from the top. Some readers will be in roles that actively contribute to strategy, while others will feel very disconnected from their organization's strategy insiders. Whatever your strategic situation and role, if you are now inspired to innovate and make money from data, you need to add discipline to your enthusiasm. If a top-down directive is lacking, then you can connect to local priorities. A vision will help you avoid monetizing data in random and uncoordinated ways, which produces convenient outcomes, not optimal ones.

This chapter will help you appreciate where your organization is heading (so you can head in the same direction). If your organization doesn't have a well-marked north star, the chapter will help you identify a data monetization direction that might work in your context. Let's begin with the research.

Four Data Monetization Strategy Archetypes

Just as personas stand in for users in product design, archetypes will be used in this chapter to represent four strategies (directions) you can take to monetize data: operational optimization, customer focus, information business, and future ready. The name of each strategy archetype sums up its distinct data monetization vision; it conveys why you monetize. Each archetype reflects different bottom-line financial priorities. For example, the operational optimization strategy prioritizes cost efficiencies, whereas the one called customer focus prioritizes finding ways to boost sales. The following sections describe the four archetype strategies. You can think of them as four quick sketches of distinct data monetization strategies.

Before jumping in, let's go over where these archetypes came from. Back in 2018, the authors surveyed 315 data leaders about their organizations' data monetization capabilities, initiatives, and outcomes. The research team clustered the respondents based on their answers to three questions about how the value they were realizing from data monetization was distributed among three categories of value realization: cost reduction, sales increase, or direct revenues from information offerings. Four statistically robust clusters emerged, and the researchers followed up with some respondents to learn more.

Figure 7.2 shows, at the top, the distribution of financial returns (cost reduction, sales increase, or direct revenues) reported by organizations in each strategy archetype.[3] The figure also includes three indices for each archetype. The first index, the Value Realization Index, is a composite score that reflects how much financial value the organization is realizing (relative to its peers). The second index, the Competitive Strength Index, was developed from five questions asking the respondents to rate the competitive distinctiveness of their products and information solutions. The third index, the Data Monetization Capability Index, shows the overall capability score for each strategy (equivalent to adding up the five individual capability scores in the capability assessment tool in the appendix).

Operational Optimization

The operational optimization strategy starts with a vision of internal transformation. About a quarter (24 percent) of the organizations in the study were categorized as having an operational optimization strategy. These organizations relied more on stripping out costs for value realization than organizations adopting any other strategy. In fact, 90 percent of the data monetization value they realized was in the form of cost savings, primarily from improving initiatives. They realized some value (7 percent of total data monetization value realized) from sales

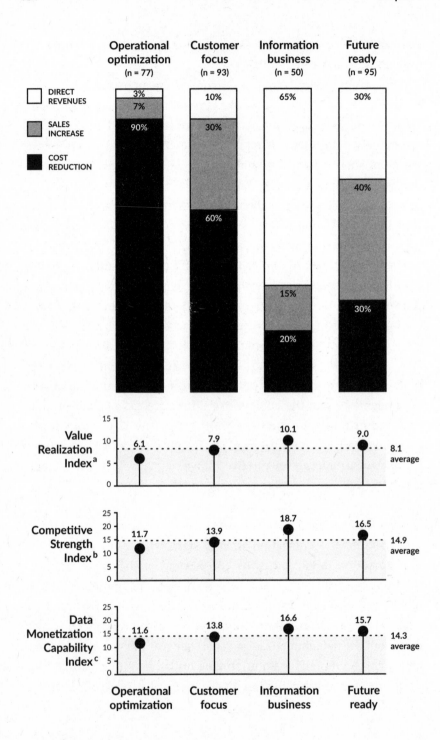

lift by making customer-facing improvements, mainly to processes that touched and mattered to customers. These organizations realized a small amount of value (3 percent) from selling (probably from selling data sets to industry data aggregators). The gains from sales lift and selling were probably incidental to the strategy.

Organizations pursuing the operational optimization strategy had the lowest Value Realization Index of the four archetypes. This no doubt reflects the challenges their leaders face in turning efficiency gains into realized value—pushing money to the bottom line. They also have the lowest Competitive Strength Index. In the past, organizations with this strategy would not have expected their internal processes to be competitively distinctive. After all, many organizations use the same off-the-shelf technology and adopt similar management approaches. But today, you can find a lot of entrepreneurial oomph in operations. Some organizations are packaging operating data or transaction data into "products" or "components" that can be easily accessed and reused internally.[4] As they begin to see opportunities to offer these data products to external users as well, the competitiveness of these products becomes more salient to them.

Figure 7.2

Key characteristics of four data monetization strategy archetypes

Notes: [a] The Value Realization Index is the sum of responses to three questions about operational efficiencies; increased product prices, sales, or loyalty; and direct revenues from selling information solutions, using a scale of 0–5, where 0 was "we do not do this" and 1–5 ranged from "very much below the average of our peers" to "very much above the average of our peers." [b] The Competitive Strength Index is the sum of responses to five questions measuring the competitive distinctiveness of wrapped products and information solutions, including whether they are first to market, groundbreaking in the marketplace, profitable, superior to those of other organizations, and highly valued by customers, using a scale of 1–5 ranging from "strongly disagree" to "strongly agree." [c] The Data Monetization Capability Index is the sum of the scores for the five capabilities. Each individual capability score is the average of responses to three items asking about practices that build that capability, using a scale of 0–5, where 0 is "we do not do this practice" and 1–5 ranges from "very poorly developed" to "very well developed."

Operational optimization strategy adopters had the lowest Data Monetization Capability Index of the four archetypes. They mainly invest in capabilities necessary for understanding and shaping operations. They generally design their organization to connect data and domain people in key business processes and core functional areas. An example of an organization that adopted this strategy is Microsoft, during the company's business model shift to cloud services, as described in chapter 3. It focused mainly, but not exclusively, on improvement initiatives to reshape its operations and create new processes and work tasks. People across the company adopted practices like dashboarding. They accessed new data assets from cloud platforms and used all five data-domain connection approaches to develop and diffuse innovations.

Does operational optimization sound right for your organization? Here are some points to consider:

- Don't discount the big bottom-line impacts that can come from adjusting and standardizing to new, better ways of work! This strategy might be an apt choice if your organization has an operating model that can scale process efficiencies across franchises, production lines, or customer touchpoints.
- If your organization is transforming like Microsoft was, the pace and expectations of an operational optimization strategy might align well. This strategy aligns nicely with investments in new, more contemporary technology and systems.
- Organizations still building foundational data monetization capabilities might find a data monetization strategy that prioritizes improving, like operational optimization, a safe way to get started with internal-facing initiatives.

Customer Focus

The customer focus strategy starts with a vision of using data to delight customers. The objective is to enhance the customer experience and serve customers more efficiently. Organizations categorized as having a customer focus strategy realized financial returns from a combination of stripping out costs (60 percent of total value realized from data monetization) and sales increases (30 percent of value realized). These organizations realize some revenues (10 percent) from charging directly for wraps as well as from selling data sets. Thirty percent of the sample fell into this cluster. Leaders guided by this strategy invest in a mix of wrapping and improving initiatives because better products and better processes are usually required to provide better service to customers.

Organizations with a customer focus strategy had the second lowest Value Realization Index of the four archetypes. Like those pursuing operational optimization, these organizations are no doubt challenged to realize value by cutting budgets. It's no less challenging for them to realize value by repricing products. However, because they realize value from both improving and wrapping, they achieve more overall value than organizations in the operational optimization cluster. Customer focus organizations also had the second lowest Competitive Strength Index. Perhaps they concentrate more of their wrapping efforts on keeping their products from being commoditized rather than on beating the competition. Over time, organizations that predominantly wrap learn that their wraps will generate larger and more lasting value if they are first to market, groundbreaking in the marketplace, profitable, superior to those of their competitors, and highly valued by customers.

Leaders at organizations pursuing this strategy invest in capabilities that support the delivery of customer-facing data and analytics at high levels of service. The average Data Monetization Capability Index for organizations with a customer focus strategy was higher than that of organizations with an operational optimization strategy. Customer-facing initiatives raise the capability bar.

Organizations with the customer focus strategy use multidisciplinary teams to connect data people with their colleagues in product management, sales, and marketing as well as with customers. These stakeholder relationships help organizations develop wrap offerings that customers will love and pay for. Chapter 4 described how multidisciplinary teams were instrumental for PepsiCo in formulating win-win customer solutions for its retail customers (and growing its joint sphere in the process). PepsiCo leaders also made good use of embedded experts. The company's Demand Accelerator put data scientists and analysts full time in marketing, sales, and advertising so the domain experts could learn data science techniques and dream up clever ways to leverage PepsiCo's extensive consumer data assets.

Does customer focus feel right to you given your organization's current direction? Here are some points to consider:

- Organizations with an operating model that requires offering a superior customer experience might find this a useful strategy.
- Organizations fighting to distinguish their products in competitive markets might find that adding useful and engaging data-fueled features and experiences might help their offerings stand out.
- Organizations that already have digital connections with customers (through an app, a website, or even a product) might find this strategy to be a good fit because they can leverage those connections to experiment and iteratively hone product features and experiences.
- Organizations eager to transition their business customer relationships into partnerships—as PepsiCo did in chapter 4—might be attracted to this strategy. As they deepen their business customer interactions and knowledge sharing, they should become better positioned to influence customer value creation.

Information Business

The information business strategy starts with a vision of using the organization's data assets to solve problems for other organizations (or consumer markets). This strategy gets people to "think like the owner of an information business" to find innovative ways to make money from data assets. Organizations in the information business cluster focused mainly on realizing value from selling information solutions (65 percent) while using wrapping initiatives to sustain the sales of those solutions (15 percent). Sixteen percent of organizations fell into this cluster (the smallest). These organizations usually focus on reducing the cost of delivering information solutions (10 percent), not stripping out costs by improving processes.

Organizations in the information business cluster had the highest Value Realization Index and the highest Competitive Strength Index of the four archetypes. Information solutions are typically high-margin offerings, and realizing value comes naturally to the leaders of information businesses. (The offerings have an explicit price tag, and customers pay it!) Leaders guided by an information business strategy develop a business model specific to selling. They quickly learn that to sustain high margins, solutions must be competitively distinct.

As you know from chapter 5, the technical and managerial requirements for selling are intense. Not surprisingly, organizations with this strategy also have the highest Data Monetization Capability Index of the four archetypes. They invest in practices, like emergent technology or sophisticated analytical techniques, that reduce the cost and time of processing heaps of data. These organizations are savvy to the core; many hire only "purple people" and then offer training and other opportunities to keep them purple. Healthcare IQ (from chapter 5) is an excellent example of a company that adopted an information business strategy (after it built up its data assets) to help hospitals cope with medical supply expenditures. Many of Healthcare IQ's staff were former hospital health spend analysts with strong analytical abilities. Like many organizations pursuing the information business strategy, Healthcare IQ drew heavily on connections that foster innovation, like embedded experts and multifunctional teams. These connections helped the company continuously develop and adapt its competitive solutions to cope with market dynamism.

Does an information business strategy appeal to you (irrespective of whether your organization would be considered an information business)? Here are some points to consider:

- Is your organization good at bringing a new product to market or at opening altogether new markets? Organizations seeking new sources of revenue and the exciting momentum of a product launch might find that a strategy focused on providing new information solutions is the right choice.

- The information business strategy can work for an organization with an incumbent business model if it is willing to start up a separate unit to nurture and develop selling-related initiatives and capabilities.
- The technical requirements and organizational commitment to deliver information solutions are no joke; selling companies like Healthcare IQ, TRIPBAM, and the other examples featured in chapter 5 use relentless innovation and deep market understanding to remain viable over time. This strategy should come with a warning label to that effect.

Future Ready

Future-ready organizations are ambidextrous: they can significantly improve their customers' experience relative to competitors while relentlessly cutting costs and simplifying their own operations.[5] Organizations adopting the future-ready strategy want to realize value from data in every way possible. A future-ready data monetization strategy inspires people enterprise-wide to be agile, reuse capabilities, seek out ecosystem opportunities, and exploit data assets. These organizations seek to be efficient and customer oriented at the same time, so they become skilled at constantly making trade-offs and adjustments.

Thirty percent of the organizations fell into this archetype. They captured financial value through cost reduction (30 percent of total data monetization value realized), sales increase (40 percent), and direct revenues (30 percent). To do this, they pursued value realization from initiatives of all three types—improving, wrapping, and selling. Future ready is by far the most difficult strategy to get right because of the need to be equally great at all three approaches. The organizations most able to pursue a future-ready strategy are digital organizations (or digitally transformed ones) and organizations that are incredibly mature in their data monetization practices. Organizations in the future-ready cluster had the second highest Value Realization Index (behind only the information business strategy) and the second highest Competitive Strength Index of the four archetypes.

These organizations also had the second highest Data Monetization Capability Index. It is mainly the desire to produce information solutions that drives the need for such strong data monetization capabilities. But excellent capabilities have a positive spillover effect in that they allow the organization to improve and wrap more effectively and efficiently. It's noteworthy that companies in the future-ready cluster had the highest score on acceptable data use capability of all four archetypes. This capability helps these organizations exploit data assets with confidence.

Leaders with future-ready aspirations work hard to establish a data democracy that allows employees far and wide to engage in data monetization initiatives relevant to their work. BBVA (from chapter 2) pursued a future-ready strategy after it added wrapping to its mix of pursuits. The company encouraged improving, wrapping, and selling, all of which could draw on a growing collection of enterprise data monetization capabilities and data assets. Like Microsoft, BBVA used all five kinds of connections between data and domain experts to facilitate widespread innovation and the diffusion of those innovations throughout the company.

Do you think your organization is primed to pursue a future-ready strategy? Here are some points to consider:

- Google and other digitally born companies pursue the future-ready strategy; their employees instinctively reach for data to solve any problem. They improve, wrap, and sell all at the same time. So, for example, developing a proposed website feature would be expected to lower cost to serve and drive more sales while contributing new data to the organization's information solutions. Organizations with this ambidextrous culture might find this strategy to be a good fit.

- The future-ready strategy requires data monetization initiative owners who can pursue goals that might normally be perceived as competing (e.g., cost reduction and sales lift). Organizations with process, product, and information solution owners who are great at experimentation and making trade-offs might find this strategy appealing.

• Organizations with robust, established governance processes and effective ways to discuss and resolve conflicting goals might find the future-ready strategy to be a good choice.

The Four Strategy Archetypes

MIT CISR researchers often compare top- and bottom-performing organizations to understand what drives success. For example, the data monetization strategy study showed that top performers in all four strategy archetypes had monetization capabilities that were just about 1.5 times as strong as those of bottom performers. Moreover, the top performers were realizing about twice as much value from data monetization as were low performers. Great capabilities are vital for achieving data monetization returns.

Your data monetization strategy should reflect the aspirations of your organization, not your industry. None of the four archetypes is aligned to any industry. In the research sample, for example, a fairly even number of financial services companies fell into each of the four archetypes (19 percent, 33 percent, 16 percent, and 32 percent, respectively), and there were financial services companies among the top and bottom performers of each archetype. That is, financial services firms can choose to compete in many different ways (by transforming their operations, by being customer-centric, by selling information solutions, or all three), and financial services firms can execute their strategies very well—or poorly.

Smart organizations do not set their strategies in stone. A data monetization strategy is a living, evolving plan that must be adapted over time to accommodate shifts in market dynamics, technology advancements (think digital), an organization's evolving capabilities, and its overarching business strategy. Thus, the data monetization strategy ideal for an organization today might not be ideal a year from now; it will need to be adjusted accordingly.

Questions to ask yourself

Which strategy archetype is the right choice for your organization now?
Which one might be the right choice in five years?

Using a Value-Effort Matrix to Select Data Monetization Initiatives

Your data monetization strategy helps establish a vision. To make progress on your strategy, you will need to make choices among the endless list of opportunities—and investments—in front of you. So, the first test of a strategy might be whether it helps you prioritize data monetization opportunities. A simple technique for doing this (an approach your organization might already use) is to array your options on a simple two-by-two value-effort matrix, like the one depicted in figure 7.3, by the value they offer and the effort they require.

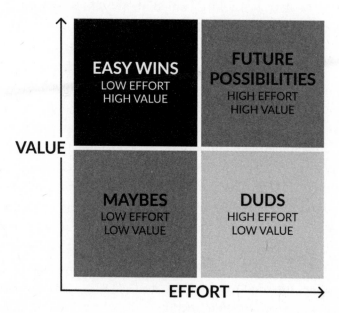

Figure 7.3
A value-effort matrix

Here are two ways to refine your use of a value-effort matrix using what you have learned about data monetization. First, define the vertical dimension of the matrix, value, in terms of your organization's data monetization strategy (or the archetype strategy that most resonates with you). Instead of arraying opportunities based on, say, projected ROI or payback period, array them on the type of value your organization's strategy targets. If your organization's strategy is operational optimization, use cost savings as the value measure. If the strategy is customer focus, use a value measure that combines sales increase and cost savings. (Just make sure, in the end, that the complete set of approved initiatives does not target only sales increases or only cost savings!) If you're pursuing an information business strategy, use revenues (direct sales and sales increases) for your value measure. If your chosen strategy is future ready, use bottom-line value realization.

Depending on your strategy, high-value opportunities (easy wins and future possibilities) might solve a costly operational workaround, they might relieve a customer pain point, or both. Low-value opportunities (maybes and duds) are simply not in line with business priorities even if they are effortless to pull off. Don't be tempted by them.

Second, adapt how you estimate effort for the horizontal dimension of the value-effort matrix. You now know that how much effort a data monetization opportunity will require depends significantly on the state of the data monetization capabilities available to your initiative teams. Data monetization opportunities that require low effort are ones for which the organization already has the necessary data assets and capabilities in place. Here's an example of a low-effort initiative: the required data assets can be accessed from a cloud platform, the team has the right data science skills, existing algorithms can be reused or adapted, customer needs are well understood, and an acceptable data use policy and procedures are not only in place but automated.

Initiatives for which capabilities are needed but not available can only reasonably be tackled in the future. But there's a silver lining: the more initiatives in that upper right quadrant (high value but high effort) that need the same data asset or data monetization capability, the more value there is in investing directly in that reusable data resource.

Another factor that affects how much effort an initiative will require is the state of your organization's data democracy. What connections exist that will help facilitate the initiatives under consideration? If the way you embed a data expert in a domain is not already established, then a lot of effort will be required to create new HR policies, work out incentive adjustments, relocate the expert, and get people used to sharing knowledge. On the other hand, if it's just a matter of filling out a form and finding a desk, less effort will be needed. Broadly speaking, less effort will be needed in those parts of an organization where data is already democratized.

In sum, your top priority initiative should be one that will add a lot of strategic value—easy money—to the bottom line and for which the data resources and organizational connections needed are already available. They are high strategic value and low data monetization effort.

As with many other estimation tools, this one is vulnerable to bias. This can be mitigated by ranking initiatives along each axis using an evidence-based approach or arriving at the location of an initiative along the axis by consensus. The value-effort matrix is an easy-to-use tool for prioritizing data monetization opportunities, especially if it is adapted based on what you know about data monetization.

The important thing is to pursue data monetization thoughtfully, have a good story to describe how things will unfold, and go after outcomes that will be valued and achievable.

Time to Reflect

A data monetization strategy indicates how an organization plans to generate its data monetization returns. It should include an organization-level view of goals, prioritized opportunities, targeted capabilities, and an ideal organizational design. The process of crafting a tailored data monetization strategy is an excellent opportunity to establish a common language regarding data across the organization. Here are the key points from this chapter to keep in mind:

- It's desirable to have a data monetization strategy that can be linked to an organization's strategy. *How widespread is the understanding of your organization's business strategy throughout the organization? To what extent do your data monetization investments reflect where your organization is heading?*

- There are four data monetization strategies that organizations commonly pursue. *Which strategy archetype is the most consistent with the data monetization strategy being pursued by your organization? Is your current data monetization strategy your organization's best choice? Looking back or looking forward, do you see this choice changing?*

- Each data monetization strategy requires different levels of capabilities. Please take the time to assess your organization's data monetization capabilities using the worksheet in the appendix if you have not already done so. *Will your capabilities support your chosen strategy? What practices does your organization need to adopt to have the capabilities it needs to support your desired strategy?*

- Organizations need to view their capabilities and connections in light of the data monetization strategy they are pursuing. *How hard is it for champions of new initiatives to predict when the capabilities they need will be available? How formalized are the connections between data and domain experts at your organization?*

You now have a vision for how you want to generate your data monetization returns, and you probably have the germ of a data monetization strategy. In the next chapter, you will learn that it's time to make it your business to monetize data.

8 Monetizing Your Data

Everybody has this idea that there is value in data, and they want to tap into it—but there is a lack of understanding of where to begin and how to get past the hype.

—Sean Cook, Pacific Life

When you head to work tomorrow, you might encounter a new data buzzword, a fascinating new data technique, a sexy new tech platform, or a colleague eager to share a shocking tweet about data. There's always something new about data to take in, something new that you need to evaluate, debate, choose, or figure out. (There are also weighty concerns outside the scope of this book that merit deep thought, like ethical AI and consumer data privacy.) You now have a starting point from which to evaluate whether something new about data is worth investigating further. You can put news about a competitor innovation, an industry shift, or a new privacy regulation in context. The data world is turbulent and entrepreneurial, always changing. Now, you should feel better prepared to get past the hype, as Sean Cook says above.

First, a very short recap of the foundational ideas presented in this book:

- Data monetization should be like every other day-to-day activity you perform to do your job. It shouldn't be seen as ambiguous or inscrutable; it is simply the act of generating financial returns from data assets. Organizations should expect an ROI from their expenditures in data assets, data monetization capabilities, data-related initiatives, and data-domain connections. Data needs to be monetized so that inflows exceed outflows.

• Data monetization comes from improving, wrapping, and selling initiatives. It requires five enterprise capabilities and thrives in organizations replete with connections between data and domain experts.

• A data monetization strategy communicates specific investment choices. A strategy helps people head in the same direction and contribute to the organization's top priorities.

Armed with this understanding of data monetization, you can engage more deeply with data-related issues and see fresh opportunities in changing circumstances. Given a chance to automate a routine process, for example, you might first ask your manager, "How are we going to cut out the slack this will free up?" When your competitor begins to package its physical product with a dashboard, you will probably ask, "What will their customers have to do to create value from that dashboard? How much value will they realize?" If a partner approaches you with an idea to cocreate a new information solution, you might wonder, "Do they have the capabilities?" And when a new privacy regulation is released, you might tap your network of "purple people," knowing that both data and domain perspectives will help to make an informed plan as to what needs to change.

The book concludes with suggested next steps for you to take: (1) evaluate the current state, (2) establish a way to track your progress, and (3) make it your business to monetize data.

Evaluate the Current State

The book's frameworks can help you take a snapshot of the current state of data monetization at your organization or within your unit or team. That snapshot can serve as your baseline. Then over time, you can measure progress against it.

Because data monetization relies on data, first consider your organization's key data assets. Does your organization have data assets that are a "single source of truth" about money, customers, employees, products, patients, legal cases, projects, or any other subject matter that is important to your organization? Are they accurate, complete, current, standardized, searchable, and understandable? With answers to these questions in mind, you can begin evaluating your capabilities, initiatives, and connections. Figure 8.1 lists the big-picture questions to ask next.

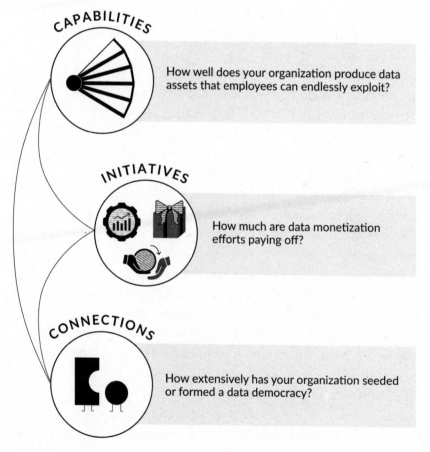

CAPABILITIES

How well does your organization produce data assets that employees can endlessly exploit?

INITIATIVES

How much are data monetization efforts paying off?

CONNECTIONS

How extensively has your organization seeded or formed a data democracy?

Figure 8.1

Assessing the current state of data monetization

How well does your organization produce data assets that employees can endlessly exploit?   Reusable data assets result from monetization capabilities, which come from your organization's data monetization practices. You can use the capability assessment worksheet in the appendix to evaluate your data management, data platform, data science, customer understanding, and acceptable data use capabilities. It will help you understand whether your practices are likely to yield capabilities (and great data assets) at all and where your capabilities are strongest and weakest. Next, consider another run-through with the worksheet to assess which practices are in place across the enterprise; get a feel for which of your organization's capabilities are "enterprise" capabilities. Those answers will shed light on how well your data assets have been set up for reuse.

How much are data monetization efforts paying off?   Most people find it highly informative, if not fascinating, to dig into the question of whether your data monetization efforts are paying off. Try to quantify the outcomes of some of your organization's recent data monetization initiatives: What kinds of value and how much value have been created and realized from improving, wrapping, and selling initiatives over the last three years? Did the initiatives achieve the sort of bottom-line returns that were expected? Were the right people held accountable for managing the risks and outcomes of these initiatives?

How extensively has your organization seeded or formed a data democracy?   To identify the "purple-ness" of your organization (where purple people can be found, where red and blue people are turning purple), evaluate your organization's data monetization connections: Of the five kinds of connections—embedded experts, multidisciplinary teams, shared services, social networks, advisory services—how many are being used in your organization? Can multifunctional teams be formed quickly, or does it take conspiring and cajoling? Are social networks being exploited to share knowledge about data problems and solutions? Are domain experts motivated to interact with and learn from data experts or not?

The objective of all this questioning is to get the big picture and food for thought. Your responses might give you confidence that your organization is on track or they might not. Just seeing how easy or hard it is to track down the answers to these questions might help you spot areas that need attention!

Establish a Way to Track Progress

You can't manage what you can't measure. As you move ahead, inspired to act and drive change, you will need a way to track your data monetization progress. You might be fortunate and work in an organization with formal data monetization monitoring or you might not. Regardless of your organization's measurement culture, the frameworks will offer guidance. Capabilities, initiatives, and connections need to be measured to some degree. If your organization already has measures to draw on, use them. If not, you will need to formulate a way to capture information about the components.

To give you a bit of inspiration, let's go back to BBVA. BBVA established a way to track its data monetization progress when it created the BBVA D&A subsidiary. The subsidiary needed to develop a formal way to monitor its financial health because it was expected to sell information solutions, self-fund its operations, and engage in financial transactions with the bank (such as paying royalties for the use of BBVA data assets). As one of her first moves, the leader of BBVA D&A developed a framework to classify projects based on their economic impact. She used the framework to evaluate what kinds of value the portfolio of D&A projects would create: some projects mainly increased sales or market size, others generated operational efficiencies, and some created nonfinancial value (such as contributing to BBVA capabilities).

Business units were accountable for creating and measuring the kind of value expected from each project they sponsored. A financial expert was hired to serve as director of finance and operations. He was responsible for managing D&A's diverse project portfolio, and he helped the business unit leaders create appropriate measurement methodologies and validate initiative outcomes. He ensured that the value created by the projects was realized for both the subsidiary and the bank.

BBVA also gave D&A accountability for building enterprise capabilities and teaching every bank employee about data science. To monitor its progress on these goals, BBVA D&A created a dashboard that tracked the unit's progress in data science capability building and talent development. The dashboard captured metrics like the number of data sets migrated from a local database to BBVA's enterprise data platform, the number of times existing algorithms were reused in new projects, and the number of BBVA employees who attended data science training. It helped subsidiary leaders identify what pockets of the bank were actively contributing to data monetization progress; they encouraged those active pockets to continue and tried to rouse other parts of the company from their inactivity.

Using this book's frameworks, you can see that BBVA tracked initiatives, capabilities, and connections. Its proprietary economic impact framework and measurement methodologies captured whether and how initiatives were paying off, which allowed the subsidiary leaders to ensure they invested in a mix of project types and that the bank gained financially from data monetization projects. Their dashboard reflected the strength of BBVA's capabilities and data democracy.

If you, too, need to craft a way to track progress, do not feel overwhelmed. There are two measurement principles to keep in mind. First, measure in a way that is not overly complicated or costly. The cost of measurement can't be greater than the value of having the measurement in hand. Ideally, organizations should measure just enough to sustain organizational commitment over time. What is "just enough" will depend on the organization's specific needs. If the investment in a process improvement is small, it might be enough to measure local efficiencies and local cost reductions or slack reallocations. If the investment is large, it might be important to surface efficiencies in downstream processes and any related slack reduction or to measure product sales lift that can be traced to the process improvement. Just be sure to say how you will verify that the money reaches the bottom line.

Second, measure in a way that will be credible to the people in your organization. Some organizations are wedded to hard evidence. They need in-depth business cases and post-audits of every investment. Other organizations need plausible evidence but are satisfied with anecdotes and back-of-the-envelope extrapolations. Still others need the ongoing production of evidence, generated by instrumentation and formalized monitoring, for value management. Only you know what builds and sustains commitment at your organization.

Make It Your Business to Monetize Data

This book has said at every turn that a lot of people in an organization need to be involved in data monetization. In fact, it argues that data monetization requires everybody. Process, product, and information solution owners must take accountability for creating value from an organization's data assets. Experts need to learn from each other and share knowledge, employees must act on insights and pursue innovations, and leaders have a duty to fund and support the effort.

Even though data monetization takes everybody, a single person (or just a few) can make a difference. The BBVA data monetization journey began with four innovators who went on a sabbatical at MIT to learn about selling information solutions. PepsiCo's Demand Accelerator might never have received funding had one seasoned and trusted sales leader not had the ear of top leaders, so he could help them see the connection between analytics and granular growth. Finally, many of the solutions and wraps that fueled Healthcare IQ's growth were proposed and championed by one customer account rep who sensed a change in customer needs and helped the company adapt its offerings and fill the need.

Now it's your turn. Right now, your organization needs people like you to get things started or keep things going. Look for opportunities to innovate with data: to improve work, enhance a product, or design an information solution. There is no better way to develop an intimate awareness of the maturity of your data monetization resources and the challenges of pushing money to the bottom line than to be part of an improving, wrapping, or selling initiative team.

So start or join an initiative team. You can begin anywhere in the value-creation process (data-insight-action), using a work challenge that you currently face. Get some data: is there an open data set (there are over three hundred thousand open data sets on data.gov) that could help you resolve your challenge? Maybe you need more insight: could you use more sophisticated number crunching? Maybe you need to standardize how you take action: would automation help? Only through doing will you truly learn how to monetize data.

Let's say you decide to tackle one of these initiative ideas. Putting together a team with all the expertise needed to launch, execute, and close out the initiative will tell you everything you need to know about your organization's data-domain connections. After you get your team together, you will need to round up the necessary data monetization capabilities. To find capabilities, you'll look for places where data monetization practices are in place; the link between practices and capabilities will become crystal clear to you. Working on your initiative, it will also become obvious why all five capabilities are needed and why it's better if capabilities are enterprise capabilities.

Assuming the initiative is a smashing success, your next learning journey will be turning the value you created into money. Your organization might have a formal process to do this, or you may need to work with many people to figure out how to make the organizational adjustments that will push money to the bottom line.

When you actively engage in data monetization, you learn and you help your organization learn. Your engagement powers the data monetization flywheel, creating momentum that initiates a positive reinforcing cycle: more data assets leading to more use, leading to more value, leading to more data assets, leading to more use, and so on. Imagine this happening across the organization as people everywhere make it their business to monetize data.

This is why data is everybody's business.

Appendix: The Capability Assessment Worksheet

The capability assessment worksheet in this appendix (table A.1) can be used to assess the data monetization capabilities of your organization and their levels (as in figure 2.3). It can also be used to calculate your organization's Data Monetization Capability Index (as in figure 7.2).

Table A.1
The capability assessment worksheet

Capability	Typical practices	Your score (0–5)	Your capability level (F, I, or A)
Data management: To build a data management capability, organizations engage in practices that turn data into accurate, integrated, and curated data assets.	**Foundational: Master data** Practices that produce reusable data assets include establishing automated data-quality processes, identifying data sources and flows that describe core business activities or key entities like customer and product, creating standard definitions of priority organizational data fields, and establishing metadata for those data fields.		
	Intermediate: Integrated data Practices that allow data to be integrated from both internal and external sources include mapping and harmonizing data sources and standardizing, matching, and joining data fields.		

Table A.1 (continued)

Capability	Typical practices	Your score (0–5)	Your capability level (F, I, or A)
	Advanced: Curated data Organizations use taxonomy and ontology to curate their data. These practices involve analyzing data and its relationships, depicting data and its relationships in a way that is accessible and meaningful to users, and maintaining that depiction over time. These practices make it possible to augment the organization's data assets with data assets from external sources or with data assets created as a byproduct of the development of AI models.		
Data platform: To build a data platform capability, organizations engage in practices that allow them to draw on cloud, open source, and advanced database technologies to produce software and hardware configurations that satisfy their data processing, management, and delivery needs.	**Foundational: Advanced tech** The adoption of cloud-native technologies is an example of a data platform practice. Modern database management tools include products that leverage leading-edge techniques for data compression, storage, optimization, and movement.		
	Intermediate: Internal access The use of APIs to offer data and analytics services internally is a practice that eases access to raw data or data assets from any system.		
	Advanced: External access APIs can also be used to make an organization's raw data or data assets available to external channels, partners, and customers. Providing APIs to stakeholders outside the organization requires adopting practices for certifying external users and tracking their platform activity.		

Table A.1 (continued)

Capability	Typical practices	Your score (0–5)	Your capability level (F, I, or A)
Data science: To build a data science capability, organizations engage in practices that advance their ability to use data science techniques and thinking. They hire new talent and upskill and develop existing employees. They invest in tools and methods that support data science work so that data science tasks can be appropriately managed and scaled.	**Foundational: Reporting** Practices that foster the use of dashboards and reporting include standardizing data presentation tools and designating which data assets will be regarded as the "single source of truth" for process outcomes or business results. They include educating employees about data storytelling and evidence-based decision-making.		
	Intermediate: Statistics Practices that promote the use of math and statistics include selecting analytics tools, hiring people with sophisticated mathematical and statistical knowledge, and establishing data science support units. They include teaching probability, statistics, and skills that increase the usability of analytics tools and techniques.		
	Advanced: Machine learning To promote the use of advanced analytics techniques such as machine learning, natural language processing, or image processing, organizations engage in feature engineering, model training, and model management. They use AI explanation practices that ensure AI models are value generating, compliant, representative, and reliable.[1]		
Customer understanding: To build a customer understanding capability, organizations connect with customers to collect data about them— demographics, sentiments, context, usage,	**Foundational: Sensemaking** Listening to customers and making sense of their needs is an example of a foundational customer understanding practice. Customer-facing employees can help organizations identify important customer needs by sharing ideas via "suggestion boxes" or crowd-sourced innovation events. These employees can also participate in agile or cross-functional teams tasked with mapping customer journeys or designing new products and processes.		

Table A.1 (continued)

Capability	Typical practices	Your score (0–5)	Your capability level (F, I, or A)
and desires—from which they extract analytical insights about core and latent customer needs.	**Intermediate: Cocreation** Engaging customers in the cocreation of new products or new processes requires practices for identifying the appropriate customer, establishing the terms of customer engagement, and making good use of customer time.		
	Advanced: Experimentation Common practices for testing ideas with customers include hypothesis testing (observing customer behavior to see if it conforms to expectations) and the use of A/B testing (using randomized experimentation with two variants, A and B).		
Acceptable data use: To build an acceptable data use capability, organizations engage in practices that allow them to effectively address regulatory and ethical concerns regarding data asset use by and about employees, partners, and customers. Organizations draw on this capability to mitigate the risk of using data assets inaccurately, undesirably, or in ways that are not contractually or legally allowable.	**Foundational: Internal oversight** Practices that ensure acceptable use of data by employees usually begin with establishing data ownership; training employees about laws, regulations, and organizational policy; setting up data access approval processes; and auditing employee data access.		
	Intermediate: External oversight Practices that ensure the appropriate use of data assets by partners begin with establishing clear agreements about appropriate use with partners and end with auditing partner use of data assets.		
	Advanced: Automation Practices that allow customers to self-manage their data begin with establishing policies regarding customer control of data. These policies are then implemented both by communicating the policies to customers and facilitating customer control through automation. Automating practices also helps organizations scale internal and external oversight activities.		

Here's how to use the worksheet. If your organization is large, with many business units, you may wish to focus your assessment on the capabilities of a particular business unit. If your focal business unit receives data-related services from a shared services or corporate IT unit, include the practices of that unit in your assessment since that unit's data monetization capabilities are made available to you.

First, score your chosen business unit on its level of adoption and use of each of the three practices within each capability. Use a scale of 0–5 (0 = we do not have this practice, 1 = very poorly developed, 2 = somewhat poorly developed, 3 = of average development, 4 = somewhat well developed, 5 = very well developed).

To assign a capability level to each asset, refer to your scores. Select the level (foundational, intermediate, or advanced) with the highest score. If you do not have a score of 3 or above for the foundational-level practices for a particular capability, that capability is not yet established. If two levels have the same score, select the higher level. For example, if the foundational and intermediate practices are somewhat well developed, and you gave those practices a score of 4 but some advanced practices have been adopted but are poorly developed, scoring 1, then the level of that capability would be intermediate. Note that the practices that build data monetization capabilities are sequential, meaning that practice scores are typically highest at the foundational level and lowest at the advanced level.

You can compare your scores to those provided by the 315 executives responding to our 2018 survey,[2] which can be found in the second table (table A.2). Note that survey respondents' capabilities were, on average, at a foundational level. To calculate your Data Monetization Capability Index, first average the three scores for each capability (the three levels). For example, if for the data management capability your foundational practices score was 4, your intermediate practices score was 4, and your advanced practices score was 1, then the average score for this capability would be 3 [(4 + 4 + 1)/3]. Then, sum up the five capability scores. The scores for this index range from 0 to 15.

Table A.2
Scores from 315 MIT CISR survey participants

Capability	Typical practices	Average scores score (0–5)	Average capability level (F, I, or A)
Data management	**Foundational: Master data** Practices that produce reusable data assets include establishing automated data-quality processes, identifying data sources and flows that describe core business activities or key entities like customer and product, creating standard definitions of priority organizational data fields, and establishing metadata for those data fields.	3.2	Foundational
	Intermediate: Integrated data Practices that allow data to be integrated from both internal and external sources include mapping and harmonizing data sources and standardizing, matching, and joining data fields.	2.9	
	Advanced: Curated data Organizations use taxonomy and ontology to curate their data. These practices involve analyzing data and its relationships, depicting data and its relationships in a way that is accessible and meaningful to users, and maintaining that depiction over time. These practices make it possible to augment the organization's data assets with data assets from external sources or with data assets created as a byproduct of the development of AI models.	2.5	
Data platform	**Foundational: Advanced tech** The adoption of cloud-native technologies is an example of a data platform practice. Modern database management tools include products that leverage leading-edge techniques for data compression, storage, optimization, and movement.	3.1	Intermediate

Table A.2 (continued)

Capability	Typical practices	Average scores score (0–5)	Average capability level (F, I, or A)
	Intermediate: Internal access The use of APIs to offer data and analytics services internally is a practice that eases access to raw data or data assets from any system.	3.0	
	Advanced: External access APIs can also be used to make an organization's raw data or data assets available to external channels, partners, and customers. Providing APIs to stakeholders outside the organization requires adopting practices for certifying external users and tracking their platform activity.	2.3	
Data science	**Foundational: Reporting** Practices that foster the use of dashboards and reporting include standardizing data presentation tools and designating which data assets will be regarded as the "single source of truth" for process outcomes or business results. They include educating employees about data storytelling and evidence-based decision-making.	3.6	Intermediate
	Intermediate: Statistics Practices that promote the use of math and statistics include selecting analytics tools, hiring people with sophisticated mathematical and statistical knowledge, and establishing data science support units. They include teaching probability, statistics, and skills that increase the usability of analytics tools and techniques.	3.1	

Table A.2 (continued)

Capability	Typical practices	Average scores score (0–5)	Average capability level (F, I, or A)
	Advanced: Machine learning To promote the use of advanced analytics techniques such as machine learning, natural language processing, or image processing, organizations engage in feature engineering, model training, and model management. They use AI explanation practices that ensure AI models are value generating, compliant, representative, and reliable.	2.2	
Customer understanding	**Foundational: Sensemaking** Listening to customers and making sense of their needs is an example of a foundational customer understanding practice. Customer-facing employees can help organizations identify important customer needs by sharing ideas via "suggestion boxes" or crowd-sourced innovation events. These employees can also participate in agile or cross-functional teams tasked with mapping customer journeys or designing new products and processes.	3.1	Foundational
	Intermediate: Cocreation Engaging customers in the cocreation of new products or new processes requires practices for identifying the appropriate customer, establishing the terms of customer engagement, and making good use of customer time.	2.9	
	Advanced: Experimentation Common practices for testing ideas with customers include hypothesis testing (observing customer behavior to see if it conforms to expectations) and the use of A/B testing (using randomized experimentation with two variants, A and B).	2.8	

Table A.2 (continued)

Capability	Typical practices	Average scores score (0–5)	Average capability level (F, I, or A)
Acceptable data use	**Foundational: Internal oversight** Practices that ensure acceptable use of data by employees usually begin with establishing data ownership; training employees about laws, regulations, and organizational policy; setting up data access approval processes; and auditing employee data access.	3.0	Foundational
	Intermediate: External oversight Practices that ensure appropriate use of data assets by partners begin with establishing clear agreements about appropriate use with partners and end with auditing partner use of data assets.	2.8	
	Advanced: Automation Practices that allow customers to self-manage their data begin with establishing policies regarding customer control of data. These policies are then implemented both by communicating the policies to customers and facilitating customer control through automation. Automating practices also helps organizations scale internal and external oversight activities.	2.3	

Note: The 315 survey respondents included executives from organizations of all sizes, with 44 percent having more than US$3 billion in annual revenues in 2017 and 32 percent having revenues under US$500 million. The majority of the executives' organizations were for profit; 42 percent were publicly traded, and 18 percent were nonprofit or governmental organizations. The organizations operated worldwide, with 79 percent having some operations in North America. The organizations competed in a range of industries; 39 percent competed in the industry categories of financial services/banking, manufacturing, and professional services.
Source: Barbara H. Wixom, "Data Monetization: Generating Financial Returns from Data and Analytics—Summary of Survey Findings," Working Paper No. 437, MIT Sloan Center for Information Systems Research, April 18, 2019, https://cisr.mit.edu/publicationMIT_CISRwp437_DataMonetizationSurveyReport_Wixom (accessed January 17, 2023).

Acknowledgments

We are grateful to the MIT Press team for their commitment and expertise. For their comments and their time, we are grateful to the anonymous reviewers and to our friends and colleagues who read early versions of the manuscript: Gregg Gullickson, Gigi Kelly, Ann Murphy, and Gary Scholten. Collaborating with our talented graphic designer Alli Torban was inspiring. Alli is patient, professional, intuitive, and creative. Alli's design process influenced our writing for the better, and her delightful graphics will help our ideas stick.

People across MIT helped shape and strengthen our ideas. Thanks to our MIT CISR colleagues for providing encouragement and incisive feedback: Isobela Byerly-Chapman, Kristine Dery, Jed Diamond, Margherita DiPinto, Chris Foglia, Nils Fonstad, Amber Franey, Dorothea Gray, Nick van der Meulen, Cheryl Miller, Ina Sebastian, Jeanne Ross, Aman Shah, Austin Van Groningen, Peter Weill, and Stephanie Woerner. Thank you to all our colleagues at the MIT Sloan School of Management, the *Sloan Management Review*, and the MIT Sloan research centers, with special appreciation to Dean Schmittlein, Michael Cusumano, Elizabeth Heichler, Abby Lundberg, and Wanda Orlikowski.

We appreciate the expertise and encouragement of the MIT Sloan Executive Education team who guided our distillation of three decades of data monetization research into a six-week, online data monetization strategy course: Isabella DiMambro, Christine Gonzalez, Peter Hirst, Paul McDonagh-Smith, Meg Regan, and the GetSmarter Team

(Cara Dewar, Andre Grobler, Pamela MacQuilkan, and John Ruzicka). These educational designers raised questions that helped us hone our content and improve its delivery. Also, we appreciate our executive education colleagues—and our colleagues in the MIT Industrial Liaison Program—for introducing us to curious global executives who actively engage with our material and help us appreciate why and how data monetization matters to leaders of all kinds.

This book reflects decades of research by a village of academic collaborators. We greatly appreciate Ida Someh's helping us understand how organizations become data democracies and what it takes to scale AI. Ida is a qualitative research guru who culled critical insights from MIT CISR interviews and case studies (including at BBVA, General Electric, and Microsoft). Thank you, Ida, for your intellectual contributions, as well as your positive attitude and your friendship. Special thanks to Ronny Schüritz and Killian Farrell for helping us understand how product managers use data analytics to enhance their offerings. Ronny and Killian are gifted data scientists who helped us develop and advance the concepts of data wrapping and data monetization capabilities. We are grateful to Gabriele Piccoli and Joaquin Rodriguez, who helped us examine data monetization using their theoretical lens of digital resources. Their collaboration has produced exciting concepts like digital data assets, actioned analytics, and data liquidity, as well as cases such as Fidelity and TRIPBAM (the latter along with Federico Pigni). Over the years, many other collaborators have generously contributed their subject area expertise to assist us with specific project needs; thank you to Anne Buff, Justin Cassey, Wynne Chin, Tom Davenport, Tamara Dull, Dale Goodhue, Robert Gregory, Rajiv Kohli, Dorothy Leidner, M. Lynne Markus, Anne Quaadgras, Paul Tallon, Peter Todd, Olgerta Tona, Hugh Watson, Rick Watson, and Angela Zutavern.

It is essential for academic work to reach—and be informed by—practitioner audiences. Thank you to the thousands of interviewees, case study participants, and survey respondents who contributed to this research over three decades. Special thanks to those leaders who allowed us to feature them in our research: Linda Abraham, Magid Abraham, Scott Albin, Elena Alfaro, Juan Murillo Arias, Sarmila Basu, Julie Batch, Tom Bayer, Marco Bressan, Mike Brown, Peter Campbell, Tom Centlivre, Michael Cleavinger, Reid Colson, Sean Cook, Jeff Dale, Norm Dobiesz, Jim DuBois, Gian Fulgoni, Danny Gilligan, Enrique Hambleton, Sue Hanson, Scott Heintzeman, Kathy Hollenhorst, Brandon Hootman, Randy Hurst, Gregg Jankowski, Vince Jeffs, Robert Jones, Nir Kaldero, David Lamond, Dick LeFave, Mike McClellan, Shamim Mohammad, Detlef Nauck, Sandra Neale, Rob Phillips, Michelle Pinheiro, Vijay Raghavan, Vijay Ravi, Jeevan Rebba, Michael Relich, Anne Marie Reynolds, Steve Reynolds, Linda Richardson, Rajeev Ronanki, Martha Roos, Marek Rucinski, Laura Sager, Kiki Sanchez, Mary Schapiro, Mihir Shah, Marcus Shipley, John Shomaker, Danny Slingerland, Tim Smith, Chris Soong, Scott Stephenson, Don Stoller, Jeff Stovall, Jeff Swearingen, Rim Tehraoui, Omid Toloui, Robert Welborn, David Wright, Jacky Wright, Bruce Yen, and Ying Yang.

We are beholden to the global leaders who fund our work at MIT CISR and participate in our research consortium. The current list of sponsors and patrons is available here: https://cisr.mit.edu/content /mit-cisr-members. Special thanks to the liaisons who provided extraordinary enthusiasm and support for our research: Nuno Barboza, Duke Bevard, Chris Blatchly, Deb Cassidy, Stijn Christiaens, Karen Clarke, Vittorio Cretella, Bernard Gavgani, David Hackshall, Alexander Haneng, Craig Hopkins, Dirk van der Horst, Naomi Jackson, Jeff Johnson, Carolyn Cameron-Kirksmith, Michelle Mahoney, Jaime Montemayor, Mark Meyer, Robert Oh, Patrick O'Rourke, Kal Ruberg, Tek Singh, Ivan Skerl, David Starmer, Jim Swanson, Bernardo Tavares, Donna Vinci, Steve Whittaker, Pui Chi Wong, and Edgar van Zoelen.

Finally, this book would not have been possible without extraordinary contributions by the MIT CISR Data Board. Since 2015, several hundred data and analytics leaders have piloted and perfected surveys, cleared schedules for research interviews and virtual discussions, debated findings, and shared struggles and wins. These lifelong learners are curious, encouraging, and enthusiastic partners who elevate our research and help move the field forward. We are grateful to every one of you. Thanks to those who helped establish the board and create a spirited community: David Abrahams, Jennifer Agnes, Laki Ahmed, Daniel Bachmann, Melanie Bell, Aurelie Bergugnat, Michael Blumberg, Gustavo Botelho de Souza, Gavin Burrows, Jonathan Carr, Licio Carvalho, Fiona Carver, Rafael Cavalcanti, Harj Chand, Krishna Cheriath, Marlo Cobb, Glenn Cogar, Scott Cooper, Tony Cossa, Glenda Crisp, José Luis Dávila, Regine Deleu, Steve DelVecchio, Jeff DeWolf, Tej Dhawan, David Dittmann, Andrew Dobson, Brad Fedosoff, Mavis Girlinghouse, Paul Grant, Ritesh Gupta, Sofia Hagström, Richard Hines, Dan Holohan, Ali Kettani, Jane King, Jim Kinzie, Joe Kleinhenz, Kate Kolich, Ram Kumar, David Lamond, Jorge Llerena, Ling Ling Lo, Gary Lotts, Andre Luckow, Esther Málaga, Jurgen Meerschaege, Malavika Melkote, Didem Michenet, Abhishek Mittal, Fredrik Ohlsson, Doug Orr, Macaire Pace, Nanda Padayachee, Ajay Padhye, Tom Pagano, Doraivelu Palanivelu, Diogo Picco, Kala Ramaswamy, Perry Rotella, Riaan Rottier, Rob Samuel, Sai Seethala, Tom Serven, Amy Shi-Nash, David Short, Fausto Sosa, Jim Tanner, Gilberto Flórez Tella, Simon Thompson, Mike Trenkle, David Vaz, Kate Wei, Greg Williams, Janine Woodside, Brett Woolley, Floyd Yager, Kelley Yohe, Brian Zacharias, and Jenny van Zyp.

A Personal Note from Barb

This book is the result of thirty years of academic research regarding a single question inspired by my doctoral work: How do organizations generate value from data? Arguably, this book is my dissertation finale! Thank you to my coauthors Cynthia Beath (known as "Boo") and Leslie Owens for helping me create a book I hope will help people reach their data dreams. I appreciate your complementary contributions, your patience, and your friendship—all of which made our collaboration a life gift.

Three influential mentors kept me on course over three decades: Hugh Watson, Ryan Nelson, and Cynthia Beath. Hugh—you inspired me to love data, appreciate practice, and make a difference in the field. Ryan—you advised me through big transitions, reminded me that fun matters, and encouraged me to reach for the stars. Boo—you saw my potential, built my confidence, and helped me touch those stars. Hugh, Ryan, and Boo, you mean the world to me.

Countless people influenced and inspired my work. I am grateful to my academic and practice friends at AIS, SIG-DSA, SIM, TDWI, TUN, and UVA's McIntire School. Special thanks to Susan Baskin, Steve Cooper, Scott Day, Alan Dennis, Howard Dresner, Jill Dyché, Wayne Eckerson, Dan Elron, Scott Gnau, Jane Griffin, Richard Hackathorn, Martin Holland, Cindi Howson, Cyndy Huddleston, Claudia Imhoff, Bill Inmon, Lakshmi Iyer, Adelaide King, Mary Lacity, Doug Laney, Evan Levy, Shawn Rogers, Anne-Marie Smith, Catherine Szpindor, Rhian Thompson, Rich Wang, Madeline Weiss, and Robert Winter.

Thank you to my family and personal friends for your love and support—and your patience and understanding—as I lean into my professional pursuits. You infuse my life with positive energy and make me a stronger and better person.

Thank you to my husband, Chris, and my daughters, Haley and Hannah. I am humbled by your unwavering love, encouragement, and humor during this book journey and throughout my professional career. Your positivity and zest for life inspire me every day. Chris, Haley, and Hannah: my heart bursts with love for you.

A Personal Note from Cynthia (a.k.a. "Boo")

When Jeanne W. Ross, Martin Mocker, and I sought feedback on early drafts of our book *Designed for Digital* (MIT Press, 2019), the most consistent piece of feedback we got was, "WHAT ABOUT DATA?" Our response was, "That's going to take a whole other book!" This is that book. I thank Barb and Leslie for the invitation to join this team, for their patience with me, and for the many, many laughs along the way. This has been an incredible journey.

Some additional thanks are in order.

First and foremost, I thank my husband, Denny McCoy. Thank you, Denny, for empathizing with my creative challenges and not trying to fix them. Thank you for helping me face up to the blank page one day before the last possible moment to begin. Thank you for teaching me to see that sometimes a piece of creative work is actually "finished." Thank you for teaching me that it is possible to be creative and disciplined at the same time. (I'm sorry I have not yet grasped the "creative and tidy at the same time" lesson.) Thank you for all the hugs and cups of coffee.

Second, I thank Burt Swanson for getting me started on this fabulous journey of research and discovery. Burt taught me to be guided in my research by relevance to practice, and that has kept my enthusiasm for research high throughout my career. He also showed me that research took a lot of pure perseverance, more rewriting than seems possible, and way more thinking than a human can tolerate. I thank him for all of that.

Third, I thank my much-missed little dog, Dolly Mama, for listening uncritically to my ranting, for being patient with me when I worked too long, and for always being up for a walk to breathe out the ideas that weren't working and breathe in some new ones.

Finally, many thanks to the universe for giving me everything I could ever want.

A Personal Note from Leslie

Thank you to Barb and Boo for inviting me into this fun and rewarding experience. I appreciate your humor, kindness, and can-do spirit.

Although this book is primarily about data, it's also about people. As I turn fifty this year, I am counting my blessings. I am lucky to have close friends from various ages and stages of my life: childhood, college, work, neighbors, and more. My mentors include Pauline Cochrane, Joe Coffey, Win Lenihan, Jeff Lyons, Stephen Powers, and Rich Strle. I am so grateful to all of you for carrying me through difficult times and helping me see and celebrate the joys and opportunities that come my way.

Thank you to my family: Mom, Dad, Adrienne, Colleen, George, Scott, Kelly, Erik, Graham, and Nick. My mom was a sensitive and smart entrepreneur who gracefully balanced home and career at a time when there were few examples out there. My dad was tenderhearted; he gave me support and confidence. My husband, Erik, and our son, Graham: you are the most precious people in my life. Thank you for giving me pep talks and perspective. You set the example for hard work and good-will that I try to follow. I love you both with my whole heart.

Notes

Introduction

1. Miriam Daniel, "Immersive View Coming Soon to Maps—Plus More Updates," The Keyword, May 11, 2022, https://blog.google/products/maps/three-maps -updates-io-2022 (accessed August 30, 2022).

2. "Alphabet Q2 2022 Earnings Call Transcript," Alphabet Investor Relations, July 26, 2022, https://abc.xyz/investor/static/pdf/2022_Q2_Earnings_Transcript .pdf (accessed August 30, 2022).

3. Barbara H. Wixom and Gabriele Piccoli, "Build Data Liquidity to Accelerate Data Monetization," MIT Sloan Center for Information Systems Research, Research Briefing, vol. XXI, no. 5, May 20, 2021, https://cisr.mit.edu/publica tion/2021_0501_DataLiquidity_WixomPiccoli (accessed January 17, 2023).

4. Barbara H. Wixom, Thilini Ariyachandra, Michael Goul, Paul Gray, Uday Kulkarni, and Gloria Phillips-Wren, "The Current State of Business Intelligence in Academia," *Communications of the AIS* 29, no. 1 (2011), http://aisel.aisnet. org/cais/vol29/iss1/16 (accessed January 17, 2023).

5. Mark Mosley and Michael Brackett, eds., *The DAMA Guide to the Data Management Body of Knowledge (DAMA-DMBOK Guide)* (Bradley Beach, NJ: Technics Publications 2009).

Chapter 1

1. Jeanne W. Ross, Cynthia M. Beath, and R. Ryan Nelson, "Redesigning CarMax to Deliver an Omni-Channel Customer Experience," Working Paper No. 442, MIT Sloan Center for Information Systems Research, June 18, 2020, https://cisr.mit.edu/publication/MIT_CISRwp442_CarMax_RossBeathNelson (accessed January 17, 2023).

2. Ida A. Someh and Barbara H. Wixom, "Microsoft Turns to Data to Drive Business Success," Working Paper No. 419, MIT Sloan Center for Information Systems Research, July 28, 2017, https://cisr.mit.edu/publication/MIT_CISR wp419_MicrosoftDataServices_SomehWixom (accessed January 17, 2023).

3. "BBVA, an Overall Digital Experience Leader Five Years in a Row, According to 'European Mobile Banking Apps, Q3 2021,'" Banco Bilbao Vizcaya Argentaria, February 11, 2022, https://www.bbva.com/en/bbva-an-overall-digital-experi ence-leader-five-year-in-a-row-according-to-european-mobile-banking-apps-q3 -2021/ (accessed August 30, 2022).

4. Barbara H. Wixom, "PepsiCo Unlocks Granular Growth Using a Data-Driven Understanding of Shoppers," Working Paper No. 439, MIT Sloan Center for Information Systems Research, December 19, 2019, https://cisr.mit.edu/publica tion/MIT_CISRwp439_PepsiCoDX_Wixom (accessed January 17, 2023).

5. Barbara H. Wixom, Killian Farrell, and Leslie Owens, "During a Crisis, Let Data Monetization Help Your Bottom Line," MIT Sloan Center for Information Systems Research, Research Briefing, vol. XX, no. 4, April 16, 2020, https:// cisr.mit.edu/publication/2020_0401_DataMonPortfolio_WixomFarrellOwens (accessed January 17, 2023).

6. Jitendra V. Singh, "Performance, Slack, and Risk Taking in Organizational Decision Making," *The Academy of Management Journal* 29, no. 3 (1986): 562–585; L. Jay Bourgeois III, "On the Measurement of Organizational Slack," *The Academy of Management Review* 6, no. 1 (1981): 29–39.

7. Barbara H. Wixom, "Data Monetization: Generating Financial Returns from Data and Analytics—Summary of Survey Findings," Working Paper No. 437, MIT Sloan Center for Information Systems Research, April 18, 2019, https://cisr .mit.edu/publication/MIT_CISRwp437_DataMonetizationSurveyReport_Wixom (accessed January 17, 2023).

8. Steven Rosenbush and Laura Stevens, "At UPS, the Algorithm Is the Driver," *Wall Street Journal*, February 16, 2015, https://www.wsj.com/articles/at-ups-the -algorithm-is-the-driver-1424136536 (accessed August 30, 2022).

9. Clint Boulton, "Columbia Sportswear Boosts Profit with Focus on Supply Chain," *Wall Street Journal*, May 8, 2015, https://www.wsj.com/articles/colum bia-sportswear-boosts-profit-with-focus-on-supply-chain-1431121627 (accessed August 30, 2022).

10. Barbara H. Wixom, "Winning with IoT: It's Time to Experiment," MIT Sloan Center for Information Systems Research, Research Briefing, vol. XVI, no. 11,

November 17, 2016, https://cisr.mit.edu/publication/2016_1101_IoT-Readiness _Wixom (accessed January 17, 2023).

11. Thomas H. Davenport and James E. Short, "The New Industrial Engineering: Information Technology and Business Process Redesign," *Sloan Management Review* (1990 Summer), 11–27; Michael Hammer, "Reengineering Work: Don't Automate, Obliterate!," *Harvard Business Review* (July-Aug 1990), 104–112; Michael Hammer and James Champy, *Reengineering the Corporation: A Manifesto for Business Revolution* (New York: HarperBusiness, 1993); Thomas H. Davenport, *Process Innovation* (Cambridge, MA: Harvard Business School Press, 1993); W. Edwards Deming, *The New Economics: For Industry, Government, Education*, 3rd ed. (Cambridge, MA: MIT Press, 2018).

12. Greg Geracie and Steven D. Eppinger, eds., *The Guide to the Product Management and Marketing Body of Knowledge: ProdBOK(R) Guide* (Carson City, NV: Product Management Educational Institute, 2013), 31.

13. Malcom Frank, Paul Roehrig, and Ben Pring, *Code Halos* (Hoboken, NJ: John Wiley & Sons, 2014).

14. "Our History," Nielsen, https://sites.nielsen.com/timelines/our-history (accessed August 20, 2022); "Our Heritage of Innovation, Transformation and Growth," IRI, https://www.iriworldwide.com/en-us/company/history (accessed February 11, 2022).

15. Anne Buff, Barbara H. Wixom, and Paul P. Tallon, "Foundations for Data Monetization," Working Paper No. 402, MIT Sloan Center for Information Systems Research, August 17, 2015, https://cisr.mit.edu/publication/MIT_CISR wp402_FoundationsForDataMonetization_BuffWixomTallon (accessed January 17, 2023).

16. "Business and Weather Data: Keys to Improved Decisions," IBM, https://www.ibm.com/products/weather-company-data-packages (accessed August 30, 2022).

Chapter 2

1. Barbara H. Wixom, "Data Monetization: Generating Financial Returns from Data and Analytics—Summary of Survey Findings," Working Paper No. 437, MIT Sloan Center for Information Systems Research, April 18, 2019, https://cisr .mit.edu/publication/MIT_CISRwp437_DataMonetizationSurveyReport_Wixom (accessed January 17, 2023).

2. Wixom, "Data Monetization."

3. Barbara H. Wixom and Killian Farrell, "Building Data Monetization Capabilities That Pay Off," MIT Sloan Center for Information Systems Research, Research Briefing, vol. XIX, no. 11, November 21, 2019, https://cisr.mit.edu/publication/2019_1101_DataMonCapsPersist_WixomFarrell (accessed January 17, 2023).

4. We initially noted the connections between practices and capabilities in our case research. We confirmed these relationships in survey research; see Wixom, "Data Monetization."

5. Barbara H. Wixom, Ida A. Someh, Angela Zutavern, and Cynthia M. Beath, "Explanation: A New Enterprise Data Monetization Capability for AI," Working Paper No. 443, MIT Sloan Center for Information Systems Research, July 1, 2020, https://cisr.mit.edu/publication/MIT_CISRwp443_SucceedingArtificial Intelligence_WixomSomehZutavernBeath (accessed January 17, 2023).

6. Barbara H. Wixom and Gabriele Piccoli, "Build Data Liquidity to Accelerate Data Monetization," MIT Sloan Center for Information Systems Research, Research Briefing, vol. XXI, no. 5, May 20, 2021, https://cisr.mit.edu/publication/2021_0501_DataLiquidity_WixomPiccoli (accessed January 17, 2023).

7. Ida A. Someh, Barbara H. Wixom, and Cynthia M. Beath, "Building AI Explanation Capability for the AI-Powered Organization," MIT Sloan Center for Information Systems Research, Research Briefing, vol. XXII, no. 7, July 21, 2022, https://cisr.mit.edu/publication/2022_0701_AIX_SomehWixomBeath (accessed January 17, 2023).

8. Barbara H. Wixom and M. Lynne Markus. "To Develop Acceptable Data Use, Build Company Norms," MIT Sloan Center for Information Systems Research, Research Briefing, vol. XVII, no. 4, April 20, 2017, https://cisr.mit.edu/publication/2017_0401_AcceptableDataUse_WixomMarkus (accessed January 17, 2023).

9. Barbara H. Wixom, Gabriele Piccoli, Ina Sebastian, and Cynthia M. Beath, "Anthem's Digital Data Sandbox," Working Paper No. 451, MIT Sloan Center for Information Systems Research, October 1, 2021, https://cisr.mit.edu/publication/MIT_CISRwp451_Anthem_WixomPiccoliSebastianBeath (accessed January 17, 2023). In 2022, Anthem Health was renamed Elevance Health (see https://www.elevancehealth.com).

10. Elena Alfaro, Juan Murillo, Fabien Girardin, Barbara H. Wixom, and Ida A. Someh, "BBVA Fuels Digital Transformation Progress with a Data Science

Center of Excellence," Working Paper No. 430, MIT Sloan Center for Information Systems Research, April 27, 2018, https://cisr.mit.edu/publication/MIT _CISRwp430_BBVADataScienceCoE_AlfaroMurilloGirardinWixomSomeh (accessed January 17, 2023). The paper was the winner of the 2018 Best Paper Competition from the Society for Information Management; "BBVA, an Overall Digital Experience Leader Five Years in a Row, According to 'European Mobile Banking Apps, Q3 2021,'" Banco Bilbao Vizcaya Argentaria, February 11, 2022, https://www.bbva.com/en/bbva-an-overall-digital-experience-leader-five-year -in-a-row-according-to-european-mobile-banking-apps-q3-2021 (accessed August 30, 2022).

11. Wixom and Farrell, "Building Data Monetization Capabilities That Pay Off."

Chapter 3

1. Barbara H. Wixom, "Data Monetization: Generating Financial Returns from Data and Analytics—Summary of Survey Findings," Working Paper No. 437, MIT Sloan Center for Information Systems Research, April 18, 2019, https://cisr .mit.edu/publication/MIT_CISRwp437_DataMonetizationSurveyReport_Wixom (accessed January 17, 2023).

2. Barbara H. Wixom, Ida A. Someh, Angela Zutavern, and Cynthia M. Beath, "Explanation: A New Enterprise Data Monetization Capability for AI," Working Paper No. 443, MIT Sloan Center for Information Systems Research, July 1, 2020, https://cisr.mit.edu/publication/MIT_CISRwp443_SucceedingArtificial Intelligence_WixomSomehZutavernBeath (accessed January 17, 2023).

3. Barbara H. Wixom, Ida A. Someh, and Robert W. Gregory, "AI Alignment: A New Management Paradigm," MIT Sloan Center for Information Systems Research, Research Briefing, vol. XX, no. 11, November 19, 2020, https:// cisr.mit.edu/publication/2020_1101_AI-Alignment_WixomSomehGregory (accessed January 17, 2023).

4. Barbara H. Wixom and Jeanne W. Ross, "The U.S. Securities and Exchange Commission: Working Smarter to Protect Investors and Ensure Efficient Markets," Working Paper No. 388, MIT Sloan Center for Information Systems Research, November 30, 2012, https://cisr.mit.edu/publication/MIT_CISRwp388 _SEC_WixomRoss (accessed January 17, 2023).

5. Barbara H. Wixom and Anne Quaadgras, "GUESS?, Inc.: Engaging the Business Community with the "New Look" of Business Intelligence," MIT Sloan

Center for Information Systems Research, Research Briefing, vol. XIII, no. 8, August 15, 2013, https://cisr.mit.edu/publication/2013_0801_GUESS_Wixom Quaadgras (accessed January 17, 2023).

6. Barbara H. Wixom, "Winning with IoT: It's Time to Experiment," MIT Sloan Center for Information Systems Research, Research Briefing, vol. XVI, no. 11, November 17, 2016, https://cisr.mit.edu/publication/2016_1101_IoT-Readiness _Wixom (accessed January 17, 2023).

7. Nitan Nohria and Ranjay Gulati, "Is Slack Good or Bad for Innovation?" *Academy of Management Journal* 39, no. 5 (1996): 1245–1264; Joseph L.C. Cheng and Idalene F. Kesner, "Organizational Slack and Response to Environmental Shifts: The Impact of Resource Allocation Patterns," *Journal of Management* 23, no. 1 (1997): 1–18.

8. "Market Capitalization of Microsoft (MSFT) June 2022," Companies Market Cap, https://companiesmarketcap.com/microsoft/marketcap (accessed June 2022).

9. Wixom, "Data Monetization."

10. Barbara H. Wixom and Killian Farrell, "Building Data Monetization Capabilities That Pay Off," MIT Sloan Center for Information Systems Research, Research Briefing, vol. XIX, no. 11, November 21, 2019, https://cisr.mit.edu /publication/2019_1101_DataMonCapsPersist_WixomFarrell (accessed January 17, 2023).

Chapter 4

1. Ronny Schüritz, Killian Farrell, and Barbara H. Wixom, "Creating Competitive Products with Analytics—Summary of Survey Findings," Working Paper, No. 438, MIT Sloan Center for Information Systems Research, June 28, 2019, https://cisr.mit.edu/publication/MIT_CISRwp438_DataWrappingParticipant Report_SchuritzFarrellWixom (accessed January 17, 2023).

2. Barbara H. Wixom and Ronny Schüritz, "Creating Customer Value Using Analytics," MIT Sloan Center for Information Systems Research, Research Briefing, vol. XVII, no. 11, November 16, 2017, https://cisr.mit.edu/publication /2017_1101_WrappingAtCochlear_WixomSchuritz (accessed January 17, 2023).

3. Wixom and Schüritz, "Creating Customer Value Using Analytics."

4. Wixom and Schüritz, "Creating Customer Value Using Analytics."

5. Ronny Schüritz, Killian Farrell, Barbara H. Wixom, and Gerhard Satzger, "Value Co-Creation in Data-Driven Services: Towards a Deeper Understanding of the Joint Sphere," International Conference for Information Systems, December 15–18, 2019; Christian Grönroos and Päivi Voima, "Critical Service Logic: Making Sense of Value Creation and Co-Creation," *Journal of the Academy of Marketing Science* 41, no. 2 (2013): 133–150.

6. Barbara H. Wixom and Ina M. Sebastian, "Don't Leave Value to Chance: Build Partnerships with Customers," MIT Sloan Center for Information Systems Research, Research Briefing, vol. XIX, no. 12, December 19, 2019, https://cisr .mit.edu/publication/2019_1201_PepsiCoCustomerPartnerships_WixomSebastian (accessed January 17, 2023).

7. "PepsiCo Annual Report, 2021," PepsiCo, https://www.pepsico.com/docs /default-source/annual-reports/2021-annual-report.pdf (accessed August 30, 2022).

8. Barbara H. Wixom, "PepsiCo Unlocks Granular Growth Using a Data-Driven Understanding of Shoppers," Working Paper No. 439, MIT Sloan Center for Information Systems Research, December 19, 2019, https://cisr.mit.edu/publica tion/MIT_CISRwp439_PepsiCoDX_Wixom (accessed January 17, 2023).

9. Margaret A. Neale, and Thomas Z. Lys, *Getting (More of) What You Want* (London: Profile Books, 2015).

10. Dale Goodhue and Barbara H. Wixom, "Carlson Hospitality Worldwide KAREs about Its Customers," in *Harnessing Customer Information for Strategic Advantage: Technical Challenges and Business Solutions*, ed. W. Eckerson and H. Watson (Seattle: The Data Warehousing Institute, 2000).

11. Barbara H. Wixom, "Data Monetization: Generating Financial Returns from Data and Analytics—Summary of Survey Findings," Working Paper No. 437, MIT Sloan Center for Information Systems Research, April 18, 2019, https:// cisr.mit.edu/publication/MIT_CISRwp437_DataMonetizationSurveyReport _Wixom (accessed January 17, 2023).

12. Barbara H. Wixom and Ronny Schüritz, "Making Money from Data Wrapping: Insights from Product Managers," MIT Sloan Center for Information Systems Research, Research Briefing, vol. XVIII, no. 12, December 20, 2018, https://cisr.mit.edu/publication/2018_1201_WrappingValue_WixomSchuritz (accessed January 17, 2023).

13. Barbara H. Wixom and Killian Farrell, "Building Data Monetization Capabilities That Pay Off," MIT Sloan Center for Information Systems Research, Research Briefing, vol. XIX, no. 11, November 21, 2019, https://cisr.mit.edu /publication/2019_1101_DataMonCapsPersist_WixomFarrell (accessed January 17, 2023).

14. Wixom, "Data Monetization."

Chapter 5

1. Anne Buff, Barbara H. Wixom, and Paul P. Tallon, "Foundations for Data Monetization," Working Paper No. 402, MIT Sloan Center for Information Systems Research, August 17, 2015, https://cisr.mit.edu/publication/MIT_CISR wp402_FoundationsForDataMonetization_BuffWixomTallon (accessed January 17, 2023).

2. "8451: Who We Are," 8451, https://www.8451.com/who-we-are (accessed August 30, 2022).

3. Barbara H. Wixom, "Data Monetization: Generating Financial Returns from Data and Analytics—Summary of Survey Findings," Working Paper No. 437, MIT Sloan Center for Information Systems Research, April 18, 2019, https://cisr .mit.edu/publication/MIT_CISRwp437_DataMonetizationSurveyReport_Wixom (accessed January 17, 2023).

4. Barbara H. Wixom and Jeanne W. Ross, "Profiting from the Data Deluge," MIT Sloan Center for Information Systems Research, Research Briefing, vol. XV, no. 12, December 17, 2015, https://cisr.mit.edu/publication/2015_1201_Data Deluge_WixomRoss (accessed January 10, 2023).

5. Buff, Wixom, and Tallon, "Foundations for Data Monetization."

6. "Global Data Broker Market Size, Share, Opportunities, COVID-19 Impact, and Trends by Data Type (Consumer Data, Business Data), by End-User Industry (BFSI, Retail, Automotive, Construction, Others), and by Geography—Forecasts from 2021 to 2026," Knowledge Sourcing Intelligence, June 2021, https://www .knowledge-sourcing.com/report/global-data-broker-market (accessed August 30, 2022).

7. "About Verisk," Verisk, https://www.verisk.com/about (accessed August 30, 2022); "Verisk Fact Sheet," Verisk Inc. Newsroom, https://www.verisk.com /newsroom/verisk-fact-sheet (accessed August 30, 2022).

8. Jennifer Belissent, "The Insights Professional's Guide to External Data Sourcing," Forrester Research, Inc., August 2, 2021, https://www.forrester.com/report/The-Insights-Professionals-Guide-To-External-Data-Sourcing/RES139331 (accessible behind paywall August 30, 2022).

9. Gabriele Piccoli, Federico Pigni, Joaquin Rodriguez, and Barbara H. Wixom, "TRIPBAM: Creating Digital Value at the Time of the COVID-19 Pandemic," Working Paper No. 444, MIT Sloan Center for Information Systems Research, July 30, 2020, https://cisr.mit.edu/publication/MIT_CISRwp444_TRIPBAM_Pic coliPigniRodriguezWixom (accessed January 10, 2023).

10. Barbara H. Wixom, Cynthia M. Beath, Ja-Nae Duane, and Ida A. Someh, "Healthcare IQ: Sensing and Responding to Change," Working Paper No. 458, MIT Sloan Center for Information Systems Research, February 1, 2023, https://cisr.mit.edu/publication/MIT_CISRwp458_HealthcareIQDataAssets_WixomBeath DuaneSomeh (accessed February 17, 2023); Barbara H. Wixom and Cheryl Miller, "Healthcare IQ: Competing as the 'Switzerland' of Health Spend Analytics," Working Paper No. 400, MIT Sloan Center for Information Systems Research, February 6, 2015, https://cisr.mit.edu/publication/MIT_CISRwp400 _HealthcareIQ_WixomMiller (accessed February 17, 2023).

11. Jay B. Barney, "Looking Inside for Competitive Advantage," *The Academy of Management Executive (1993–2005)* 9, no. 4 (1995): 49–61.

12. Magid Abraham, "Data Monetization Strategies That Can Show You the Money," MIT Sloan Center for Information Research, MIT CISR Summer Session, June 18, 2014.

13. Barbara H. Wixom, Anne Buff, and Paul P. Tallon, "Six Sources of Value for Information Businesses," MIT Sloan Center for Information Systems Research, Research Briefing, vol. XV, no. 1, January 15, 2015, https://cisr.mit.edu/publica tion/2015_0101_DataMonetizationValue_WixomBuffTallon (accessed January 10, 2023).

14. Barbara H. Wixom and Killian Farrell, "Building Data Monetization Capabilities That Pay Off," MIT Sloan Center for Information Systems Research, Research Briefing, vol. XIX, no. 11, November 21, 2019, https://cisr.mit.edu /publication/2019_1101_DataMonCapsPersist_WixomFarrell (accessed January 17, 2023).

15. Barbara H. Wixom and M. Lynne Markus, "To Develop Acceptable Data Use, Build Company Norms," MIT Sloan Center for Information Systems Research, Research Briefing, vol. XVII, no. 4, April 20, 2017, https://cisr.mit.edu

/publication/2017_0401_AcceptableDataUse_WixomMarkus (accessed January 10, 2023); Dorothy Leidner, Olgerta Tona, Barbara H. Wixom, and Ida A. Someh, "Make Dignity Core to Employee Data Use," *Sloan Management Review*, September 22, 2021. Reprint #63215.

Chapter 6

1. Ida Someh, Barbara H. Wixom, Michael J Davern, and Graeme Shanks, "Configuring Relationships Between Analytics and Business-Domain Groups for Knowledge Integration," *JAIS Preprints* (forthcoming), http://aisel.aisnet.org /jais_preprints/63 (accessed January 17, 2023).

2. Someh, Wixom, Davern, and Shanks, "Configuring Relationships."

3. This thought experiment is inspired by events at a conference that Barbara Wixom attended years ago hosted by TDWI (Transforming Data with Intelligence), an education and research provider. Data leaders invited to the conference were encouraged to bring an executive business champion. At the start of the conference, the data leaders received a red shirt and the business champions received a blue one. At the end of the conference, everyone left with a purple shirt.

4. Ida A. Someh and Barbara H. Wixom, "Microsoft Turns to Data to Drive Business Success," Working Paper No. 419, MIT Sloan Center for Information Systems Research, July 28, 2017, https://cisr.mit.edu/publication/MIT_CISRwp 419_MicrosoftDataServices_SomehWixom (accessed January 17, 2023).

5. Ida A. Someh and Barbara H. Wixom, "Data-Driven Transformation at Microsoft," MIT Sloan Center for Information Systems Research, Research Briefing, vol. XVII, no. 8, August 17, 2017, https://cisr.mit.edu/publication/2017_0801 _DataDrivenTransformation_SomehWixom (accessed January 17, 2023).

Chapter 7

1. Donald C. Hambrick and James W. Frederickson, "Are You Sure You Have a Strategy?" *The Academy of Management Executive* 19, no. 4 (2001): 48–59.

2. Wayne Eckerson, *The Data Strategy Guidebook: What Every Executive Needs to Know* (Boston, MA: Eckerson Group, 2019).

3. Barbara H. Wixom, Killian Farrell, and Leslie Owens, "During a Crisis, Let Data Monetization Help Your Bottom Line," MIT Sloan Center for Information

Systems Research, Research Briefing, vol. XX, no. 4, April 16, 2020, https://cisr.mit.edu/publication/2020_0401_DataMonPortfolio_WixomFarrellOwens (accessed January 17, 2023).

4. Veerai Desai, Tim Fountaine, and Kayvaun Rowshankish, "A Better Way to Put Your Data to Work," *Harvard Business Review* (July-Aug 2022), 3–9.

5. Stephanie L. Woerner, Peter Weill, and Ina M. Sebastian, *Future Ready: The Four Pathways to Capturing Digital Value* (Cambridge, MA: Harvard Business Review Press, 2022).

Appendix

1. Ida A. Someh, Barara H. Wixom, and Cynthia M. Beath, "Building AI Explanation Capability for the AI-Powered Organization," MIT Sloan Center for Information Systems, Research Briefing, vol. XXII, no. 7, July 21, 2022, https://cisr.mit.edu/publication/2022_0701_AIX_SomehWixomBeath (accessed January 17, 2023).

2. Barbara H. Wixom, "Data Monetization: Generating Financial Returns from Data and Analytics—Summary of Survey Findings," Working Paper No. 437, MIT Sloan Center for Information Systems Research, April 18, 2019, https://cisr.mit.edu/publication/MIT_CISRwp437_DataMonetizationSurveyReport_Wixom (accessed January 17, 2023).

Index